National Writers Series
2023 LITERARY JOURNAL

Copyright ©2023

National Writers Series

Published by National Writers Series
3301 Veterans Drive, Suite 214
Traverse City, MI 49684
All rights reserved.
ISBN: 978-1-958363-94-2

Printed in the United States of America
Cover Art: Jack Bidwell
Book Design: Andrea Reider
Book Production: Mission Point Press
www.missionpointpress.com

For additional copies, please visit
nationalwriterseries.org/raisingwriters

Cover Art: *Collision 1* by Jack Bidwell

Cover Design: Andrea Reider, Designer for Mission Point Press

Editor: Ari Mokdad, Education Director for National Writer Series

2023 Cover Artist

Jack Bidwell is a student at Grand Valley State University who is studying art and marketing. He is thrilled to have his work included as the cover art for this year's NWS Literary Journal. You can see more of his art on instagram @jack.bidwell. showcase

> Note to Reader:
> Some of the works in the *National Writers Series 2023 Literary Journal* may not be appropriate for a younger reading audience.

National Writer Series

2023 Literary Journal

CONTENTS

XV   INTRODUCTION

1   Flash Fiction for Middle Schoolers
2023 Class

2   INSTRUCTOR INTRODUCTION: FLASH FICTION FOR MIDDLE SCHOOLERS
Karin Killian

3   SNAKE EYES
Kent Gardner Dickinson, 7th grade

4   SPARROW AND MOUSE: A STORY ABOUT HOME
Eliana Koller, 6th grade

6   FOOTSTEPS ON THE MOUNTAIN
JuJu Pine, 6th grade

8   KAILANI'S ADVENTURE: PART I
Sophie Schopieray, 6th grade

15   Novel Writing Program at West Middle School
2022-2023 Class

16   INSTRUCTOR INTRODUCTION: NOVEL WRITING PROGRAM AT WEST MIDDLE SCHOOL
Jacque Burke

17   BOOK BLURB FOR CHAMPION
Sophia A. Eustice, 7th grade

18   BOOK BLURB FOR THE FUGITIVE PRINCESS
Abigail Reding, 6th grade

19 DEMONS IN THE DAHLIAS
Azraeya Dunham, 7th grade

23 WHAT THE ROAD WILL BRING
Mateo Nash, 6th grade

29 TADL's NWS Novel Writing Program
2022-2023 Class

30 INSTRUCTOR INTRODUCTION:
TRAVERSE AREA DISTRICT LIBRARY'S
NWS NOVEL WRITING PROGRAM
Jacque Burke

31 THE CURSED SPARROW
Ingrid Waldron, 6th grade

37 EXCERPT FROM DIVIDED WE FALL
Jack Hennessy, 8th grade

42 DENDRITIQUE
Mina Cotner, 10th grade

51 Front Street Writers Manistee
2023 Class

52 INSTRUCTOR INTRODUCTION:
FRONT STREET WRITERS MANISTEE
Lauren K. Carlson

53 TO WRITE
Lola Piper, 12th Grade

54 PANIC, STRESS, TALK
Grace Condon, 8th Grade

55 SO I THOUGHT
Grace Condon, 8th Grade

56   **THE VOICE**
Thomas Racine, 6th Grade

57   **SCHOOL CLOCKS**
Alexis McClellan, 8th Grade.

58   **SOMEDAY I'LL LOVE LOLA PIPER**
lola piper, 12th Grade

59   **REASONS WHY YOU ARE A GREAT MOTHER**
Lola Piper, 12th Grade

60   **THINGS THAT ARE UNSAYABLE TO YOUR MOTHER**
Lola Piper, 12th Grade

61   **THIS IS NOT ABOUT A LABEL**
Lola Piper, 12th Grade

62   **OLDER BUT NOT WISER**
Leah McClellan, 8th Grade

63   **THINGS I FOUND IN THE ABANDONED SCHOOL**
Jacob Szynski, 6th Grade

64   **THE FIRST DIVE**
Marlee Hamilton, 6th Grade

66   **KINDERGARTEN LOVE**
Marlee Hamilton, 6th Grade

67   **THE DAY I GOT MY DOG (IN 2 PARTS)**
Leah Szynski, 6th Grade

69   **EXPLORING**
Jacob Szysnki, 6th Grade

70   **OLD MANISTEE HIGH SCHOOL**
Jonas Carlson, 6th Grade

75	Front Street Writers Creative Writing Lab Grand Traverse 2022-2023 Class
76	**INSTRUCTOR INTRODUCTION: FRONT STREET WRITERS CREATIVE WRITING LAB GRAND TRAVERSE** Kevin Fitton
77	**FLOOD OF THE WHITE WALL** Sela Geraci, 12th grade
87	**EXCERPT FROM US** Delaney Cram, 12th grade
95	**ROARING AUGUST** Tess Tarchak-Hiss, 9th grade
103	Writers Studio 2022-2023 Class
104	**INSTRUCTOR INTRODUCTION: WRITERS STUDIO** Teresa Scollen
105	**THE JOY OF BEING HIDDEN** Minnie Bardenhagen, 11th grade
110	**EGO EGO** Sydney Boettcher, 11th grade
112	**BOX** Reegan Craker, 11th grade
113	**RED IN THE WATERCOLOR PALETTE** Alister Easterwood, 12th grade
114	**EXCERPT FROM NOVEL: *DROWNING*** Marisa Marshall, 12th grade

117   **FORGOTTEN BLADE**
Randale McCuien, 11th grade

118   **ODE TO THE DOVE THAT FLEW AWAY**
Lucas McSwain, 11th grade

120   **THE REAL NOURISHMENT OF CHILI CON CARNE**
Dominic Montoya-Arlt, 11th grade

123   **THE DARK RIDE**
Mason Moran, 11th grade

125   **BEFORE AND AFTER**
Abraham Murphy, 12th grade

127   **COFFIN THOUGHTS**
Eli Pszczolkowski, 12th grade

129   **A LUMPY BEET**
Vincent Redman, 11th grade

131   **LOVE IN A DIFFICULT TIME OF BISCUITS: WHY THE LITTLE THINGS MATTER**
Madeline Rowney, 11th grade

135   **THE STORY OF NOTHING, SOMETHING, AND THE BEGINNING**
Isabel Schmidt, 11th Grade

137   **FREE FALL**
Megan Speers, 12th grade

139   **THRONE**
Alicia Streeter, 11th grade

154   **ALL ALONE**
Yahir Torres, 12th grade

155   TIME AT THE CORE
Gabrielle Vermilya, 11th grade

158   THE LIFE OF A GLASS CONTAINER
Aubrey West, 11th grade

162   Building Stories
2023 Class

163   INSTRUCTOR INTRODUCTION: BUILDING STORIES
Karin Killian

165   THE PAINTER'S PORTRAIT
Liam Faunce, 9th grade

169   BURNING ICE
Kristen May, 11th grade

173   NWS Scholarship Winners and Honorable Mentions
In partnership with the Grand Traverse Regional Community Foundation

174   INTRODUCTION FROM GINA THORNBURY
Grand Traverse Regional Community Foundation

175   WHAT IS YOUR PURPOSE?
Navaeh Wharton, 12th grade

181   THE MOON AND BACK
Lucy Ettawageshik, 12th grade

186 **HARBORING HOPE: TAKING A LOOK AT HOMELESSNESS IN TRAVERSE CITY THROUGH THE LENS OF ONE ORGANIZATION, SAFE HARBOR**
Lucy Poppleton, 11th grade

189 **FINDING REFUGE**
Kristen May, 12th grade

192 **THE VALUE OF THE UNKNOWN**
Isabelle Keely, 11th grade

196 **DREAMS OF HOME**
Taqwa Totakhail, 11th grade

199 **"AMONG THE WILDFLOWERS" AFTER KEVIN YOUNG**
Megan Speers, 12th grade

201 **GHAZAL WITH BUBBLEGUM AND BUZZING DOWNWARD THOUGHT SPIRALS WITH LYRICS FROM MARINA**
Eli Pszczolkowski, 12th grade

203 Contributors

221 Acknowledgements

Introduction

The National Writers Series (NWS) is a year-round book festival held in Traverse City, MI. Although we are well-known for hosting world-class and best-selling authors from around the globe, our mission is to support young writers by offering free creative writing classes to our region.

Each year, NWS showcases the work of our Raising Writers and our Front Street Writers programs. This year, we expanded our reach to the Manistee community, and we are proud to feature these wonderful middle school and high school students in the *National Writers Series Literary Journal*. This year, we have also included students from the Writers Studio at the Northwest Ed Career Tech. It is with great pleasure that we have assembled this journal and we celebrate the students commitment to the literary arts.

You'll find stories, essays, poems, a play, and excerpts from novels written by students throughout their courses and semester-long studies. NWS has been honored to work alongside some of our regions best creative writing teachers who have devoted their time, energy, and compassion in mentoring students towards their creative dreams.

NWS is dedicated to building the skills of our future storytellers, poets, playwrights, and more. We are looking forward to continuing our educational offerings and are grateful to the countless individuals who have helped make this journal possible. These free creative writing classes would not be possible without the support and dedication of our community. If you are interested in supporting our programs, please contact NWS Executive Director Anne Stanton at director@nwstc.org. You can find more information about our classes, scholarships, and more at nationalwritersseries.org.

–Ari Mokdad, Education Manager for NWS

Flash Fiction for Middle Schoolers

2023 Class

INSTRUCTOR INTRODUCTION: FLASH FICTION FOR MIDDLE SCHOOLERS
Karin Killian

The art of fiction requires awareness and imagination. In this class we began by discussing essential elements of a story—character, plot/problem, point of view, setting and voice—then we read and discussed exemplary flash fiction pieces by other writers, studying specifics of their construction. However, all this theory and observation is useless if we can't put pen to page and create a first draft. Writers build confidence when they avoid slipping into the rut of overthinking. And the best way to do this is to trick ourselves into quickly drafting one story after another after another. Thus, I love to teach young writers to focus on the fantastic fun that can be had in the process of making up a story.

We focused on fun in this short flash fiction course by playing lots of generative writing games. Some, like "The Name Game" we played together. In The Name Game, one writer makes up an impromptu character description, then we quickly name the character together, describe their appearance, then decide where they live and what is happening in their life in the moment of the story. The kids loved this game so much, we often played four rounds in a row, each of which created an entire story draft in less than five minutes. Next, we had timed writing sessions, during which the students took inspiration from the stories we constructed together and wrote drafts of their own, in five minutes. We shared our drafts by reading them out loud to each other. (Yes, I did the exercises too!) Finally, we experimented with switching up certain craft elements of our drafts, to see what would change when we consciously shifted methods of story construction. It was particularly lovely to witness these young writers' expanding awareness of how switching point of view or verb tense can quickly alter a story, even opening up portals to new information and awareness that was not present in the first drafts.

The middle school writers who took this class all have *fantastic* imaginations, and they inspired me with their energy, excitement and creativity.

SNAKE EYES
Kent Gardner Dickinson, 7th grade

Clip-clop, clip-clop. Hear that folks? That's the sound of Davey Hendrickison, more commonly known to the authorities as "Snake Eyes." He's riding his faithful steed across Oklahoma to pillage old man Pickle Bob's camp, which by the way has a vault with $50,000 and a massive armory. Luckily, Davey took the finest bounty hunters to raid the property. Some came for the guns, others for the profit. But, there's a little conundrum... escaping with a rusty revolver pointed to your forehead. Or more simply, getting out alive.

SPARROW AND MOUSE: A STORY ABOUT HOME

Eliana Koller, 6th grade

My tree. That pretty much summed my life up. It was my home, my friend, even my birthplace. I would fly and spin up to the topmost branches, picking the sweet red cherries as I went. There was a bed, a chest for my things, and a table for food. The tree was my home. All I needed.

Until humans came to destroy it.

I stuck my head out the door. It was a beautiful summer day; the wind was blowing gently and the gossipy robins (Kiwi, Feather, and Charlie) were chirping. Perfect to go splashing in the river near my tree. I shivered in anticipation, then sat down to a breakfast of oats and cherries. Suddenly, the tree shivered. It wobbled a little. I squawked and flew out the door, determined to find what was causing this. Underneath the tree, there was a whole gathering of "hoomins." With sharp things. *Chopping down my beautiful tree.*

I screeched with alarm and dive-bombed one hoomin, then kept kicking and flapping in their faces, desperately trying to save my home. But it was too late. In just a minute, my tree, no, my *entire existence,* lay in the dust at my feet. Raindrops started falling, reflecting my mood, and the hoomins started running for shelter.

Shelter I didn't have anymore. I knew I'd better pack up, but I didn't move. I couldn't just accept that it had happened.

That's why I wasn't paying attention when the cat came.

Ring-a-ling. Ring-a-ling. A bell tinkled softly, but I didn't move. It was probably just a hoomin coming back. But I did turn around to look at a bush. Was it...moving? Suddenly, a cat jumped out of the bush and slowly stalked towards me. "Lookee here, a treat for old Stan has come. You're a little morsel, but I'll make do." The cat walked leisurely towards me; he must have known I couldn't fly. I braced myself, closing my eyes. This was the end of my life. I never even got to find another house! Suddenly, a gray blur streaked across my vision. "Leave it alone, Stan! Firstly, it's not your food, and secondly, I *believe* I told you to STAY OUT OF MY YARD!" the gray creature roared. Unbelievably, the cat hissed, cursed, and turned tail and fled. I was super surprised. How had this creature saved me in such few words? I turned to thank it, when I stopped short. "Why, you're just a mouse!"

"Wrong. I'm a mouse that just saved your feathery hide. Now my warning applies to you too, so scram! We don't need folks thinking..." He walked away to his home under a tree stump, me following him frantically. "Wait! Wait! I need a home to stay in..." The mouse stopped and stared at me a bit, judging me.

"...Fine. My name's Pritchard. But you'll have to work to stay here."

The next month was amazing. I slowly warmed up to Pritchard, and vice versa. In the mornings, we talked and sipped elderberry tea, and in the evenings, we sat by his carefully monitored fire (We were in a forest, after all) and roasted cherries.

One evening, we were sitting near the river and watching a beautiful sunset. "Why were you so desperate for shelter that day?" Pritchard asked suddenly, jolting me. "Oh. I guess...I just wanted a home. Where I could belong. My books never judged me." We sat there, thinking. I got up to go to bed, but the mouse stayed. He said, "You know, there's a saying my ma used to tell me. 'Home is always where your loved ones are, not just a bed or books.' Do you get that?"

"Yeah, Pritchard," I said, sitting back down. "I guess now I'm home."

FOOTSTEPS ON THE MOUNTAIN
JuJu Pine, 6th grade

"Run!" Screams a high-pitched voice. "Run Sammy!" The voice yells again.

"Get out of here!" Now the voice had a face. She was probably about 13 with shoulder length, buttery blond hair, olive green eyes, and a huge, bloody scrape and an unforgettable look of terror and pain.

"Run Sam!" The girl says again, as she starts to run. Now there's a second girl who appeared out of a very tiny cave. The new girl is about the same age and average height and has long, flowy, chocolate brown hair and oddly colored, light purple-ish pink eyes. She obeys the command.

They are running as fast as they could down the stunning —slightly snowy— mountain. A few seconds later the blonde girl trips on a rock as the mountain rumbles and shakes. As she is getting up she sees a small cave in the mountain just big enough for both girls to fit.

"Sam!" She yells, pointing to the cave. "There!" The dark-haired girl sprints to the blonde, running twice as fast now, and pulls her up. Together the girls bolt in to the cave. Sam — the dark-haired girl — makes it first. "Come on Nailah!" Sam encourages, "Hurry!"

Nailah is almost to the cave when the mountain rumbles again, knocking her back at least three feet. Now the mountain is rumbling every few seconds. Almost like — footsteps? Sam runs out of the cave to help Nailah, but before she gets there someone new appears. Someone who pushes Nailah right off the edge of the mountain. The person runs off to the side and disappears into the snowy mountain air, as if they were never there.

"NOOOOOOO!" Sam yells, racing to the edge of the cliff. "No." She's whispering now, spotting Nailah's bright blue designer boot. Which isn't the only thing she sees. There's also a pair of legs and lots of red.

Blood.

Sam is overwhelmed with rage and fury. Who would do this?

Suddenly, she hears a twig snap behind her. She turns and sees a figure in a black hoodie duck behind a tree. She does not see their face, but when they speak, the voice sounds oddly familiar. "I've waited so long for this." It says.

The next thing Sam knows, she too is falling, falling, falling.

KAILANI'S ADVENTURE: PART I
Sophie Schopieray, 6th grade

Preface

"The sea is too strong, Kailani!" Josefine hollered at me. I looked back at her, paddling desperately in the raging seas. One more giant wave, and she would be gone. *I* would be gone. "I'm sorry, Josefine," I called. After a sorrowful glance at her, I paddled away, ready to take on anything that came at me.

Chapter One

"Kailani!" Mr. Ray hollered at me. I snapped my head up from my sea coral desk, noticing all the other turtles staring at me. Apparently I had been asleep, but this definitely wasn't the first time it had happened. Mr Ray looked unimpressed. "Since *someone* wasn't paying attention during this period, your assignment tonight is to study the importance of algae," he announced. I sighed in annoyment, but algae wasn't the end of the world. And I was sure the whole class knew that as well. Homework in Mr. Ray's class can just be a sentence and you'd get full credit. Of course, I always went the extra mile in writing an essay. Suddenly, the shell rang. The class plummeted out of Mr. Ray's room for home. I grabbed my seabooks off my desk and paddled out as soon as the parade had died down. "Kailani!" a voice shouted. I looked around, but the other turtles around me were minding their own business. I decided it could've just been my imagination, until someone yelled my name again, but louder. I stopped in my tracks and stood to the side of the halls, just until the person yelling my name spotted me. Soon, I found a turtle swimming frantically around the hallway. Josefine. She glanced my way and basically flew to me. "Whoa!" I told her. She seemed to listen to me, and closed her eyes in a calm surrender.

Chapter Two

I watched as tears fell from her face. "What's wrong?" I asked. She handed me a piece of seaweed. An "F" covered the page. Josefine never got F's. She would be the last person in my family to. Josefine was the brainiac and I was the bubble-head. "How?" I asked her. Using her flippers to wipe away her tears, she uttered, "M-Madame Anemone told us t-to study moon jellies, and you know I'm afraid of them, so I-I didn't do the project."
I knew how afraid of moon jellyfish Josefine was, but just not doing the project? That didn't sound like her at all. But I decided to let it go. I grabbed Josefine's flippers and flung her onto my back. If I wanted her to cheer up, this would be the way.
"Ready," Josefine announced. I took her signal and swam off into the ocean for home.

Chapter Three

As I was paddling home, I noticed bigger waves than usual. I dove underwater to dodge them, but it was no use for a small turtle like me. Josefine tumbled off my back and whirled in circles. I was rushed forward by the force of the wave and backflipped my way into a coral reef. I tried with all my might to bust my way out, but after 5 minutes of injuring my flippers, I gave in. The coral was wrapped all around me, like it was saying, 'There's no point in trying to escape'. I took the coral's imaginative advice and rested. Josefine was shaking her head, trying to relieve all the dizziness. She glanced my way and gaped at the sight of me. She rushed over, wanting to help. "There's no use," I confessed
"What are you going to do, sit here all night?" She questioned.
I rolled my eyes in annoyance, but that was actually what I was planning to do.
A few hours later, I noticed a figure swimming near us. I glimpsed over at Josefine, who was sleeping on top of coral. "Josefine," I whispered, "Josefine!"

She stirred a bit, but then fell back to sleep. As the figure was getting closer, I recognized the shape. It was another turtle! I wiggled my body, attempting to get out of the grasp of the evil coral. The coral moved a bit, but not enough to free me. The turtle was now 8 feet away, and I recognized them. It was my mother.

Chapter Four

"What in the name of tarnation are ya doing, stuck in that coral?" She exclaimed. I admired my mother's southern accent, but sometimes it got on my nerves.

"There was a big wave, Momma, and it flung me in here," I replied.

She sighed and lifted her flippers to untangle me. As soon as I was free, Josefine started to wake up. She lifted her head and scanned the ocean. Once the drowsiness had left her, she noticed mother. She sped to her side and grasped her in a bear hug. "You girls must be tired and hungry!" mother declared. Josefine and I nodded our heads and jumped up onto her back. She swam to the surface, hoping to find the glow of the moon jellyfish, our favorite snack. Josefine realized we were looking for them, and started to whine. She hates moon jellies, but it doesn't stop us. As we reached the surface, I knew for a fact that no moon jellies would be on our menu tonight.

Chapter Five

The waves raged. They could kill little turtles like Josefine and I. The sky, I had never seen so dark. Lightning crashed onto the waters, ready to strike out anything that goes near it. Mother flashed a worried face at us, and I could see why. A humongous wave was headed straight for us. We held on to our mother's shell for dear life, as the wave was only a few feet away. Josefine started sobbing, and muttering prayers to the Sea Goddess, Amphitrite.

I set my head down onto my mother's shell. I was ready for whatever comes our way. "Hold on, girls," Mother whispered. The wave was now rushing above us. As Josefine muttered her last word, I held onto her flipper. The wave pushed Josefine and I far underwater, the wave pressing down on us. Water started to flow down my beak. I gasped for air, but it was no use. I closed my eyes, and images of death filled my mind. I went deeper into the images, hoping to find something happy. "Kailani," a faint voice called, "Kailani!" Before I had the time to respond, everything went black.

Photo by Jonas Carlson

Novel Writing Program at West Middle School

2022-2023 Class

INSTRUCTOR INTRODUCTION: NOVEL WRITING PROGRAM AT WEST MIDDLE SCHOOL

Jacque Burke

Aspiring writers from Traverse City West Middle School met weekly throughout the month of October 2022 to learn about and plan a novel. Utilizing resources from National Novel Writing Month's (NaNoWriMo) Young Writer's Program, students learned about world-building, plot development, creating rich characters, magic systems, and story structure. Then in November, these amazing students endeavored to write their novel with a specific word count goal in mind. Our students wrote more than 153,000 words during the month through in-class writing challenges and nightly writing sprints via the chat server Discord. In addition to writing, they offered one another support and praise throughout the month to help keep the motivation going. Several stayed connected after November in order to finish their novels and edit their submissions. Their stories are exciting, imaginative, magical, and emotional. Working with these amazing kids was often the best part of my week, and my hope is that they not only had fun working on their novels but also found a community of other writers that they can turn to when they need inspiration and support.

BOOK BLURB FOR CHAMPION

Sophia A. Eustice, 7th grade

16-year-old Claire Hawthorn is living in an orphanage in the Upper Peninsula of Michigan in 2003 with only a few memories of her parents before their untimely death. Memories of a baby brother from her childhood when her parents were alive haunt her, but there is no record of another child anywhere. Claire, who is already struggling with her emerging bisexuality, questions the memories of her life before the orphanage and has convinced herself she imagined the child. At least for now but she can't ignore the nagging feeling deep down that something is missing from her life.

13-year-old Harry Jones is living in Norwich, England, with his adopted mother and father with no recollection of his life before them, except for one of his mothers, at least he thinks it's his mother. With a graveyard next to his house, he is weirdly drawn to it. Specifically, the one labeled Alexander and Miranda Hawthorn. Why is he drawn to the grave? Who were they? Did he know them before he was orphaned?

When the two meet they realize that the mystery of their past is more complicated than they thought.

BOOK BLURB FOR THE FUGITIVE PRINCESS

Abigail Reding, 6th grade

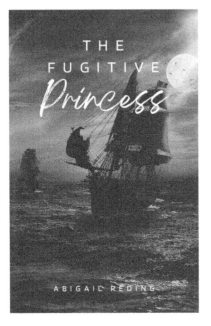

Princess Lani was only nine years old when her life turned upside down. Her kingdom was conquered by the Nation of Kistaro, and she was sent away for her own safety. For the last five years, she has been hiding on a prison island among thieves and criminals, learning to blend in with them and defend herself. Though she's scared for her parents, Lani has grown used to this life and its hardships.

Meanwhile, the new rulers of Algrana have not forgotten about Lani, and finally found where she has been hiding. Desperate to escape, she and her guards take passage on a smuggler's ship, searching for somewhere else to hide. But nowhere seems to be safe for them anymore. Lani gradually begins to realize that she'll never be able to evade her pursuers for long and that her kingdom is desperately in need of a revolution.

But Lani will find it harder and harder to find allies in her frightened kingdom full of spies and soldiers. Everyone she knows is in danger just from being near her. Along with some unlikely allies, she has no choice but to attempt the impossible. Crossing a deadly forest of carnivorous plants, befriending hardened smugglers and criminals, and confronting her own shattered past, all to reclaim her crown. Lani has never been under this much pressure before, and this worried fourteen-year-old starts to wonder how much more she can take before it breaks her.

DEMONS IN THE DAHLIAS
Azraeya Dunham, 7th grade

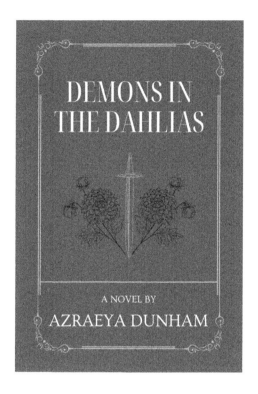

CHAPTER ONE

The shadows lingered through the lifting night sky, and the wind fluttered through the bedroom, sending a shiver down my spine. I took a deep breath of the morning air, the scent of lilacs wafting soundly through it. I stumbled out of bed and into new clothes. I walked toward the children's bedrooms, stopping to watch them wistfully before I went to wake them.

"Good morning, Father," Alexander spoke, eagerly awaiting his breakfast as his sister Liana slowly arose to get ready for school.

"Will Mother be home soon?" Alexander questioned through a mouth full of food. My mouth tipped into a tight bow, creasing my grin ever so slightly.

"Your mother is still gone. I understand, though. I miss her too."

"Oh," Alexander remarked, disappointment plastered on his face.

I turned back to the sink. I, too, wished for my wife back. Around a year ago, she had been drafted into the army to fight an opponent. The only problem is no one knows who these "opposers" are; only those dying for the cause will know. I shifted my weight as I dried the newly cleaned dishes and put them in the cupboard. I had been so deep in thought I didn't even notice my daughter hugging me goodbye. I was missing so much these days. I kept wandering into the crevices of my mind trying to make sense of this world. Everything seemed off, nothing quite set into what it should be. Nothing seemed... permanent.

A shriek from the nursery broke my train of thought. I went to pick up my youngest daughter from the small bed she lay in.

"My dear Emily,"- I started with a hush of love in my voice-" whatever ails you?"

She looked at me quizzically, a wide grin spreading across her initially fear-stricken face.

"Scary," she whispered, the sunlight reaching through the nursery shining upon her golden curls and lighting up the room.

"Ahh, well, it wasn't real, darling, and nothing will hurt you. I've *got you*."

She snuggled closer to my chest, her dazzling eyes watching my every move. I inhaled deeply, trying with all my might to keep my tears from breaking through the barrier that was my mask. *They mustn't see my sadness"* was my motto to shield my children from the very real possibility of something I did not dare consider. My *children* leaving me. If my wife did not return from duty within the next year, I would have to meet with the Higher Jury, and they would discuss the placement of my children.

The thought burned through my mind and seared me, allowing a single tear to reach my cheek and roll down my forlorn face. As I wiped it away, I heard a knock at the door. Setting Emily back in her bed, I ventured to the door and composed myself before opening it.

I opened the door to see two women, one of whom was my wife's friend and the other an acquaintance from my wife's military training camp years back. This visit was not unusual, but it was oddly suspect.

"Ah, Maryetta and Sarah, to what do I owe this pleasure? Please come in."

The women bowed, removed their hats, and hurriedly entered the house. Once they had settled, they still seemed uneasy. I noticed it as they sat down. *Perhaps some good hospitality is key,* I thought to myself.

"Would either of you like a cold beverage?"

They both nodded solemnly. I slowly took this into account. I grabbed a glass for each of them, filling each as my mind moved a billion miles an hour.

My wife's closest friend, Maryetta, sighed. "We have some bad news David," Maryetta said quietly as if afraid to speak. However, Sarah was not.

"Your wife has sadly perished in battle." Maryetta gave Sarah a grave look.

I froze, the glassware trembling in my hands. I couldn't breathe or think. I felt the glass slip through my hands as I sank to the floor, the darkness clouding my eyes, the pain cutting at my heart with every beat, then it all went black.

CHAPTER TWO

The light of the chandelier dazzled the eyes of onlookers as they walked through the ballroom. I sat frozen in my seat as I awaited the most beautiful woman I'd ever seen in my life. My eyes followed her glory as she flowed down the stairs in a satin gown. This scene was surreal, exactly as I had remembered meeting my wife. Too surreal.

She broke into a run at the bottom of the stairs. When she finally reached me, the vision changed. The satin dress was now covered in blood, her face went white with fear as she cried for me to save her. Her eyes were bloodshot, and tears painted her face. I tried to move, but I was frozen. I tried to reach her with every muscle in my body. Tears started to flow freely now. When I could finally move, I launched myself at her but she disappeared into a mist. I turned to find her. Nothing. The room had gone black. Her voice echoed through the darkness, "HELP! SAVE ME!DAVID! DAVID, IT HURTS."DA-" her voice choked off as light filled the dark room, bringing me back to reality.

The light of the tincture maker's office filled the room. I shot up, immediately worried about my children. Had they seen the interaction with the soldiers? Where was Emily? How long had I been out? This question finally brought to my mind the weirdly familiar dream. I shuddered at the thought of it; it had felt so real. After I had convinced the midwife of my health, she let me go home. My daughter, Liana, was waiting for me in the dining room with yet another new book to read. As I walked through the threshold, a shiver was sent down my spine. It seemed tainted with the horror of my nightmare. I continued walking through the house and set my hat on the table. I froze. Something had clicked in my mind, something I hadn't thought of before. Without giving it a second thought, I collected all my children and walked them to their Aunt Cathy's house. After dropping them off, I made an arrangements with a local farmer to use one of his finer horses. I had found out what my dream meant. I didn't know why I knew or if I was even right. All I knew was that even if she was dead, I was going to find my wife, and there was nothing anybody could do to stop me.

WHAT THE ROAD WILL BRING
Mateo Nash, 6th grade

Six years after the death of his wife, Bard Oakely woke up one morning to find his only child, a son named Ralos, missing and a note telling him that he had been kidnapped. Dismayed at losing another family member, he set out to look for him immediately, going into the massive Vast Forest to do so. There, he was caught between a dragon and its gold horde, a situation very difficult to negotiate, and was attacked. Nearly dead, he was saved by a friend, Tom Falcon, who had followed him through the forest, and together they fought the beast off. The two companions then continued their adventure together, their hopes higher than ever before. They have just finished preparing a duck that they hunted.

    The duck was superb, though they wasted several good hours preparing it. By the time they finished breakfasting, the sun had climbed high into the sky and the birdsong, light and beautiful, had resumed. But this time around, Bard had someone to share in the brilliant sights and sounds, and no monstrous dragon to ruin it. A swift-flowing stream, gleaming in the sunlight, ran through the path, filled with clear, cold water. Here they had a drink and filled their water skins before sitting down in the shade of a particularly large tree to talk and do other things of the sort.

"So!" Bard began, after a long and rather awkward silence. "What do you think of our, well, *grand adventure*, I suppose you could call it?"

Tom barked a cold laugh. "'*Grand adventure,* eh? That's not the first name that came to my mind for it!" Bard laughed, and another silence ensued.

"Anyways," Bard said finally, "we had better get moving again. We've rested here for far too long." Tom agreed, so they packed up (though there wasn't much to pack) and left.

It was dusk once more before they stopped again, and Tom was suddenly struck with a terrible thought. Why hadn't he thought of this *earlier?*

"Did you bring a tent?" he asked Bard frantically. An amused look came over Bard's face.

"Of course so. Do you think me a fool? Although, now that I think of it, I do not see yours. You did bring one, did you not?" he said.

Oh, um, yes, well, that is to say, that–no," he said awkwardly. "No, I did not." Bard sighed.

"Ah well, I suppose we'll have to make do without. My tent could maybe fit two if we really tried. Here, take a blanket." He handed one to Tom. Now Tom felt really very foolish, and his face flushed an intense shade of red, though he doubted his companion would notice in the dimming evening light.

"Sorry, I–" he began.

"No need to apologize." Bard kicked around to find a good spot to settle down for the night. "We all make mistakes at times. Some of us more than others ...." A dark shadow passed briefly over his face, as if he were remembering some unpleasant event, but it was over as swiftly as it had come, and he soon resumed his search.

That night, eerie noises came from all around, and after a half-hour of listening to them, they decided to have a night watch.

"I'll have the first shift!" cried Tom, eager to make his friend happy at least once that day. But he did not know that Bard was very grateful to have him along: he had been lonely without a companion and would not have made it out of the dragon situation without him.

"Alright," Bard said, yawning. "Awaken me when my shift has come." And he fell asleep. Tom, however, was wide awake and very alert. No sight got past him, no sound unheard by his ears and unfiltered by his mind. He watched and waited, waited and watched for something, *anything* to happen. But when Bard's shift came, and Tom's wish remained ungranted, having only seen a few coyotes and heard the hoots of a lonely owl, a heavy frustration fell upon him. It had been hours, and he was tired at last, but perhaps he should wait a little longer just in case. A little longer would do no harm. Then he would awaken Bard. And so Tom continued watching and waiting, until finally he fell into a deep slumber. And so it was that he never heard the bushes stir…and never saw something emerge from them.

The next morning as Tom awoke, he saw that the hedge was covered with blood and that Bard was missing. He panicked immediately.

"No, no, no! Where *has* he gone?" He searched everywhere, but it seemed to be in vain, until at long last he came upon a trail of blood. It was very subtle, with only small puddles here and there, this way and that, but it was unmistakable. He tracked it down into a clearing in the forest, where he found a handkerchief with *BO* inscribed in its bottom-right corner. *Bard's* handkerchief.

"Oh, no! What–what happened to him? No, no, no!" He frantically searched the ground for more signs of his friend but found none, save the puddles of blood that littered the forest floor. He followed the trail once more, this time at a far quicker pace, coming across several random items that he took to be Bard's. A piece of torn cloth, a pocket watch, a compass, and a sword. The sword, in fact, he knew to be Bard's, as it had been hanging over the mantelpiece every time he visited his house. He grabbed it, in case it was to be needed, and hurried along.

Finally, he came upon a clearing in the forest, and what he saw frightened him. It was the dragon. The Dragon hated Bard with a fearsome passion, and had dragged him from the hedge to the riverside where he was now. He could have killed Bard easily, and his friend, too, but no, he wanted Bard to suffer, suffer until he could bear it no longer, and then he would die. The dragon could go back for the friend later. And so it was that Tom found Bard, hanging from the great beast's jaws, with a lifeless look in his eyes. He was so horrified that for a moment he couldn't move, couldn't speak, couldn't do *anything*, but then his senses returned to him, and he rushed to his friend's aid.

The dragon opened his mouth to roar in anger and Bard's body, well, he hoped he wasn't a *body* yet, dropped to the ground. Tom leapt aside as the dragon spewed fire and remembered the weak area under the wing that Bard had stabbed in their previous battle. He rushed forward to attack, but the dragon had expected this and swung its great tail at Tom. He was hit, and he fell back, bloody (for one of its tail spines had stabbed him) and with the breath knocked out of him. He staggered to his feet, wincing, only to dive aside again to avoid another round of the beast's scorching breath. Sweat and blood stained the ground around him, both from him and Bard, but he kept fighting, barely avoiding death, but never quite reaching the dragon's weak point. Finally, the inevitable occurred, and the great claws raked across Tom's chest He fell back, unable to fight any longer. His enemy pinned him to the ground under a heavily-scaled paw. The dragon bent his head low to whisper one final thing into Tom's ear, something he had said the first time they had met:

"*Krang-frask, falgrock*.' 'Farewell, human.' There was no one to help him now. So as the flames that would end him sprang from the dragon's jaws, he thrust his sword upward, and prepared himself, if any there were, for the next life.

When Bard awoke, well, he was very surprised that he had *awoken* at all. He could vaguely recall rising before the break of dawn and encountering a huge, red dragon as soon as he opened his eyes. There was a struggle, long and hard, for Bard now knew of his fierce adversary's weak spot, but Bard lost his sword and was dragged away. The last thing he remembered was the great beast closing its jaws upon him, and then all was dark. Now, as he staggered to his feet, he was much surprised (and rather delighted) to see his enemy lying dead in a puddle of blood not a hundred paces away. But as he walked over to the enormous carcass, a sight met his eyes that grieved him deeply. Tom. There he lay upon the ground, his body charred and unmoving, his ears unhearing, his eyes unseeing. Dead, dead for all the world. Dead.

He saw that his sword, wielded in Tom's hands, had slain the beast, penetrating its skull straight through the roof of its mouth.

"Farewell, my good friend!" he whispered shakily, retrieving his sword from Tom's charred, lifeless hands. Tears streamed down his face. "May you be avenged many times over, and may your memory never fade!" He sheathed the sword and said no more, only wept softly as he turned to march off into the forest and continue his adventure, alone once more.

TADL's NWS Novel Writing Program

2022-2023 Class

INSTRUCTOR INTRODUCTION: TRAVERSE AREA DISTRICT LIBRARY'S NWS NOVEL WRITING PROGRAM

Jacque Burke

Aspiring writers in grades 6th-10th met weekly as part of the Youth Services Department of the Traverse Area District Library's novel writing program. Throughout the month of October, they learn about and plan a novel. Utilizing resources from National Novel Writing Month's (NaNoWriMo) Young Writer's Program, students learned about world-building, plot development, creating rich characters, magic systems, and story structure. Then in November, these amazing students endeavored to write their novel with a specific word count goal in mind. Our students wrote more than 110,000 words during the month through in-class writing challenges and nightly writing sprints via the chat server Discord. In addition to writing, they offered one another support and praise throughout the month to help keep the motivation going. Several stayed connected after November in order to finish their novels and edit their submissions. Their stories are exciting, imaginative, magical, and emotional. Working with these amazing kids was often the best part of my week, and my hope is that they not only had fun working on their novels but also found a community of other writers that they can turn to when they need inspiration and support.

THE CURSED SPARROW
Ingrid Waldron, 6th grade

Prologue

    A cloaked figure hurried through the shadowy, empty streets, carrying a bundle of blankets in her arms. She looked around nervously, searching for any guards that could be hiding in the shadows waiting to ambush her and stop her escape. There were no guards she could see, so she continued her mission, hoping the guards would not show their faces at all.

    The distant sound of music and laughter reached her keen ears, and stopping for a moment, she looked down at the higher rings below. The streets of Ring Four were lit up slightly more than the streets of the ring she was currently in. She could make out a lit patio suspended over the edge of the ring below, the source of the music and laughter. Tiny black shapes danced around one another, swaying to the beat of the lively music. *Idiots! Even if they were favorites, the government won't protect them from today!* She thought to herself, frowning.

    She glanced up at the giant clock tower that sat in the center of the city and could be seen from all rings. 1:48. It was almost time. If the people partying didn't flee to safety soon, they would end up dead. She might end up dead, too, if she didn't start moving faster.

    The bundle in her arms squirmed around and wailed, sending a jolt of alarm through her body. "Shhh, darling, it's going to be okay, you'll be safe soon…" She cooed, wrapping the blankets slightly tighter so that the small child inside the blankets could not squirm as much, and brushed a white strand of hair from her child's face and hugged the bundle closer to her chest. *I hope that's true,* she thought privately, gently rocking the bundle back to sleep. The cloaked woman looked around quickly, then started walking quickly down the ill-lit street.

    She sped up her pace more, almost jogging through the silent streets. Everyone up here in Ring 5 knew to hide on this day. They knew what to expect. Every year, the impact on Ring Five was the most devastating for those who ignored common sense. *Like me,* she reminded herself. She swerved into an alleyway, the one that led to the safety and freedom she needed. Once she was fully into the alley, concealed by the shadows and her cloak, she glanced over her shoulder at the clock.

Her heart almost stopped. 1:56. Four minutes left. In the shadows in the doorways lining the side of the stone wall that surrounded the whole city, she could see the glowing blue masks and white wings that foretold the coming tidal wave of death soon to strike the city. She quickened her pace even more, desperate to get to the end of the alleyway, to the ladder that was waiting for her. She changed her pace into a full jog, as she very carefully, for fear of dropping the precious bundle of blankets, which held the person that meant more to her than life itself.

She was a few feet away from the ladder when the clock chimed 2:00.

Booooooooooooooong.

Booooooooooooooong.

The clock reverberated through the paved street. The thumping of feet alerted the coming of the "angels". She wished she could fly, to stretch her wings, skip the ladder, and escape the death and misery that hung over the cursed city. But, to fly was to commit suicide. Being seen had the same effect. If she did either of those things, she would end up dead before she could even blink. She ducked into some boxes lining the walls of the alleyway as the sound of thumping feet echoed through the alleyway, becoming louder and closer with every second. She drew in her breath to control her panicked breathing, hoping the boxes, her dark-colored cloak, and the shadows would be enough to conceal her.

The pairs of heavy footsteps continued. But, to the cloaked women's horror, a pair of heavy footsteps turned into the alleyway she was hiding in. It slowed to a walking pace as it neared the end of the alleyway and the cloaked women's hiding spot and then stopped. Directly in front of the boxes. Despite the shadows surrounding her, she glimpsed the angle's hulking shape, the broad wings upon its back. Even without seeing the true colors of the angel's wing through the white painted over them, she knew what it was. *A hawk!* She thought, horror flooding her body. *Nonononononononononono!* Hawks were bad news. *Very* bad news. There was silence as the hawk stood completely still. The cloaked woman could imagine it sniffing the air like a hound, searching for her blood.

The bundle in the cloaked women's arms twitched and awoke from her slumber at the worst possible time. *Don'tspeakdon'tmakeasounddon'tcrybequietpleasepleaseplease!* The cloaked woman willed her child silently. For a second, the silence continued, and she thought it had worked, that her pure will had silenced her child.

"FOO DA!!" shrieked the child at the top volume.

Of course... Just my lousy luck! the cloaked woman muttered inwardly to herself. The Angel turned its horrible, ugly, masked face to the boxes where the cloaked woman and child hid. The angel's halo lit-up, and its gray mask glowed, bathing it in an eerie blue light, illuminating its white-painted wings.

Suddenly, fast as lightning, its arms shot out, tearing the boxes apart and revealing the cloaked woman tightly holding the squirming, hungry bundle to her chest. She knew what was coming next, even before the Angel raised the wickedly sharp spear that was aimed at her heart. A split second before it came down, she twisted her body so her back was to the angel, protecting her bundle. She felt the spear rip through her flesh and bone, then felt it as it pierced her heart. She never knew it would hurt this badly, never expected it to feel like fire was burning every fiber of her being. With her last, dying breath, she curled her body further around the bundle.

Goodbye, Wren... she thought.

And then, with a soft *woosh* the breath drifted from her body, the darkness closed in, and she was gone.

Chapter 1
16 years later...

I watched as the rest of the "angels" filed through the death-ways. When I was younger, I named the doorways lining the wall that surrounded our city "death-ways" because" the "angels" brought death with them, and they entered and exited through these doorways. This year's execution day had only killed about 12,900 people. That was a small amount compared to the population of our city Huevo (Way-VO). Think of the biggest number you can. I bet that's not even close to the population of Huevo. There are *way* too many people for one "small" city. It didn't help that our government wouldn't let anyone leave. Still, the government could have come up with a better solution to population control than having the Exterminators kill as many people as they possibly could in one day each year. The Exterminators were nicknamed "angels" because they had their wings dyed white and blue halos hovered above their heads to show that they were alive.

Blood and dead bodies were everywhere, and so were small, traumatized children. The government didn't even bless us with their wonderful presence to help us clean up. Also, to produce and train more Angels, they kidnapped our children at the age of five and made them bloodthirsty lunatics. Ah yes. They, the government, call our city "The beautiful heaven in a world of darkness." I think it's more like *we're* the World of Darkness.

A voice cuts through my thinking, breaking me out of my little trance.

"Wren..? Where are you?" I hear Nettie call.

I sigh. Time to come out of hiding.

Over the years, I have found multiple hiding spots to hide from society and to hide on execution day. I crawled out of the pile of debris, wincing as a small, pointy rock stabbed my knee. My current hiding spot used to be a house, but it collapsed a year ago. It didn't look comfortable enough from the outside to be a hiding space, but inside I laid down a blanket and made it acceptable.

As soon as Nettie saw me, she raced over and hugged me tightly. She was my adopted mother. My parents both died to the Angels. My dad died protecting my mother as she gave birth, my mom trying to…I don't remember exactly what. I just know Nettie found her dead body in an alleyway, curled around me, and holding me tightly to her chest. Apparently, I was really, *really* hungry.

I also know that Nettie feels partly responsible for their deaths. I don't know why. I *do* know she knows about what my mom was trying to do.

And that she helped. Also, I know that she has always been a family friend. That's a fact I know.

"Wren?" Oops. Sometimes I get lost in my thoughts. "Are you ready to help us clear the bodies?" Nettie asks me, looking me in the eye.

Ah, yes. Time to drag the dead bodies into a pile. I have no grudge or disrespect for the dead. Or for blood. It's just that it's hard to watch other people mourn and hug the ones they love, those who survived. I just really wish my mom and dad didn't die and that they were still here. I wish I had blood relatives to be with.

Stay in the present, Wren.

I followed Nettie to the streets and located the nearest body. Oh, joy. Time for some heavy lifting of a cold, lifeless person that weighs as much as twenty bricks. I put my arms under the armpits of the dead person, dragging them to the slowly growing pile of bodies in the middle of the road. Why in the middle of the road? Because, of course, we want people to be stopped on their way to work to pay respect to strangers they don't even know or don't care about! Kidding. It's because we don't have anywhere else big enough for the number of dead.

There are about twenty people dead on our street. It seems disrespectful to drag all of them into an alleyway for the rats. I go for the body of a little girl who lived down the street selling papers on the corner, pick her up, throw her over my shoulder, and dump her on the ever-growing pile. She'll be missed, but someone else will replace her. We finish cleaning up the street and gather around Nettie.

"Well done, everybody." Nettie congratulates us.

"Why do we have to do this?" sniffled Abby. She's one of Nettie's daughters and my adopted sister. Poor kid. She had *just* turned six, the age that Nettie made you help with the bodies. It's a perfect way to traumatize a child!

The families of the lost gathered around the pile of bodies, mourning. Nettie and the other adopted children gathered around the bodies to pay their respect. A few wandered off to get food and water and clean up. I always found it awkward to pay respect to the dead bodies of people I had never known. I didn't know what to do, and just standing there looking awkward was not something I wanted to do. I turned to the only reasonable option–running. Or, more accurately, flying.

"Going to take a short flight!" I yelled over to Nettie, and before she or anybody else could stop me, I was airborne, my rounded light brown wings beating the air to keep me aloft. I glided a third time around my ring, observing the activity below me.

Our city is made of five rings, not including the capital, which sits at the lowest part of the city. Our city is shaped like an egg. The more powerful the ring is, the lower it is. I live in ring five, the dirtiest and most disgraceful ring. Nobody wants to live here. However, it's the closest to the outside world.

Unfortunately, it's also closest to the force field. The force field is a huge dome on the top of the city, caging us in and keeping the acid rain out of Huevo. It can kill you if you fly too high. Or shock you. Or just push you backward. It depends on what mode it's on. Currently, it's in clear mode, meaning you can't see the force field until you get close to it. This is the best mode that I know of. It's better for curious, tiny people. It also means we can fly super high, which is what I am doing right now.

I flapped my wings harder and harder, stretching my hand up, up, up until it brushed against the force field. It shoved me back, pushing me down lower. Since I couldn't hover like a hummingbird, I moved in tiny circles, looking out at the outside world I would never be able to experience. A sea of pink-leafed trees spread as far as my eye could see, covering the ground, their thick trunks winding up. The forbidden books said that all of them had a way of killing you. Acid sap, poison gas, chainsaw vines. I don't know how the books would know that.

I stared up at the sky, watching the clouds inch across the sky. The sun shone down, and I basked in the little warmth it brought me. I stayed there for a while, just watching the clouds and looking out at the pink rainforest. This was my favorite spot in the whole city. Soon, my wings got tired, and I was forced to return to my ring, to my waiting adopted family, and to a worried woman with a tear-stained face.

EXCERPT FROM DIVIDED WE FALL
Jack Hennessy, 8th grade

Chapter 1
Carolina Waters

The sun was setting on the fallen empire for the 14,807th time.

The shining celestial orb bled red and orange across the blue South Carolina sky, giving the impression of a vibrant watercolor painting reflected beautifully in the gentle ocean tide below. You could still make out the toppled statues and ghostly pavilion through the dark water, remnants of a better time when children would run around in the park while their parents talked with one another at a park bench, not a care in the world. But now, a lone person sat on top of the stone wall preventing downtown Charleston from flooding, watching the fish circle around a rusted statue of some man they would never know.

A click of a button was heard as a small dolphin jumped into the air about fifty feet away before falling back into the salty water with a splash. She pulled what looked like a small, hard piece of paper out of a black camera, setting the camera down on the rough surface of the wall and holding the paper up to the setting sun. Before long, an image of the soaring dolphin appeared, frozen forever on the glossy surface of the Polaroid film.

She tucked the camera and photograph into a small satchel that hung from her narrow shoulders, taking one last look at the ghost of what used to be the seaside part of the "Battery," as the elders in the city called it. Then, she slid down the wall, satchel bobbing as she hit the sidewalk below.

She swept her hair out of their eyes, revealing eyes the color of the coffee that the wealthy drank with every meal. Her hair, which was the color of a ripe tangerine, went down to just below her shoulders, where it curved slightly at the tips. She had a somewhat narrow nose, a distinct chin, and thin lips that curved into a smile as she turned to face the sunset. She wore a stained blue dress that went down to halfway between her knees and ankles, blowing backwards towards the city.

After a minute, she turned around to face downtown Charleston before breaking into a run. She ran past a long-abandoned church, past the fenced-off row of rainbow houses, past the dimly lit bakeries, until she was in front of a run-down gelato shop near the college, its fading sign starting to splinter. She took off the satchel and gripped it in her left hand, fingers curled around the leather strap. She approached the dark blue door quickly and twisted the golden doorknob, pushing the heavy door behind her.

She slowly walked into a dark room containing two small, charcoal, hand-patched couches pushed against the side of the wall and a small grey counter that used to house different flavors of gelato. A dented oven and a rusting sink were visible behind it, dirty dishes piled in the latter. She made a quick dash to the grey set of doors to the left of the counter and quietly pulled the left one open, only to stop in her tracks as she looked at the woman standing just behind the doors.

She was a large, strong woman with greying blond hair pulled back into a tight bun. She wore a tight navy shirt and ripped, dirt-covered jeans that looked like they hadn't been washed in a couple of weeks.

"Valorie," she said in a strict voice. "Were you out at the wall again?"

"No," she said. "I was at the college helping Uncle Simon with some stuff he needed to move out."

"So, when I talk to him tomorrow, he will say you were with him?"

"There's no need for that, you know he's busy with the end of school," Valorie said quickly.

"I'm sure he won't mind. It will only take a minute," the woman said.

"Fine," Valorie said curtly, "Now let me go to my room. There are better things I could do with my time than chatting with my mom."

"Alright," her mother said, narrowing her pewter grey eyes, "Simon can fill me in tomorrow since you won't."

"Yes, he will," Valorie shouted as she dashed past her mother and into a small room to the right, slamming the wooden door behind her.

Valorie quickly pulled something from her satchel before tossing it on a hook on the wall. Sighing, she threw herself onto the too thin bed that rested against the far end of the room.

She held up the object she had taken from her satchel: a small, boxy phone with a tough back that had what looked like three flames in front of one another with the words *Trimagma Industries* inscribed below the flames. She clicked the screen of the phone and watched it light up, glowing dimly in the dull lighting of the room.

Hello VALORIE SPARKS. Please confirm your identity with Fingerprint Identification, it read. Valorie rested her right index finger upon the center of the screen, which bore a small green circle with a red, blue, and yellow fingerprint on it that contrasted with the dark grey background. *Thank You* the screen showed as it changed from a plain grey to a bright white with black words scattered across it.

A small box on the top left of the screen read *V Sparks's Essay 7*. Valorie couldn't be bothered with a title. She scrolled down to the bottom of the screen where a bold *B-* was plastered right below the end of the essay. *Not bad*, Valorie thought. Her history essay from last year had received a D.

Bored, Valorie scrolled back to the top and reread the summary she had been forced to write:

The country of South Carolina originally started 486 years ago as the British colony of Carolina. It would eventually split in two, South Carolina taking the south side and North Carolina controlling the north side. It would go on to declare independence from Britain in 1776, along with twelve other colonies. They would wage war against Britain and become independent a few years later after a British surrender.

These colonies would go on to form the United States of America, which remained whole until 1860, when South Carolina would once again declare independence, this time because of the election of Abraham Lincoln, who opposed the spread of slavery. The remaining states in the southern half of the United States would go on to also declare independence and form the Confederate States of America, which would declare war against the United States in 1861 at the now underwater Fort Sumter off the coast of Charleston. The South would eventually lose this war and rejoin the Union a few years later and South Carolina's economy was hurt badly after the war, as Lincoln had banned slavery, the state's primary source of income.

The United States would involve itself in a few wars over a couple of centuries, but none would hurt more than World War Three. The world's largest nations would fight in a nuclear war in 2074 that would result in all involved countries being quarantined from the rest of the world. The United States would suffer greatly from this, and in 2109, the fifty states would split into independent countries, though many would remain very close to their fellow ex States.

South Carolina is currently a strong ally with North Carolina and Georgia. Today, South Carolina's economy has improved, and has become the wealthiest state south of Virginia and east of Texas, mainly due to the wealthy abandoning Florida and relocating here and Georgia following the rising sea level that has flooded coastlines across the country.

Valorie yawned. She couldn't think of anything more boring except perhaps last year's project on the "economy." Valorie rolled her eyes. Nobody but the rich kids at the political university in Columbia had any reason to care about how much money gas costs. Valorie's father had gone to South Carolina State Political University, hoping to one day become Governor. He had a promising start, getting top grades, winning the "Most likely to become Governor" section in his senior yearbook, and getting elected to the South Carolina House of Representatives, but it all came to an end at the site of Fort Sumter five years ago when Valorie was ten. She tried to forget about it and think about something else, the summer, dinner, anything else, but the memory of her father's death replayed itself in her head for what felt like the millionth time.

DENDRITIQUE
Mina Cotner, 10th grade

In the midst of a war of succession, the son of a Marquis goes to prison for a murder he claims to have not committed and meets a peasant who will challenge his worldview; the victim of a self-inflicted curse meets a promising peer. DENDRITIQUE is a novel set in an analogue to Earth around the early fifteenth century. Beginning in a jail cell, it follows in parallel the journeys of Ferre Hornblende and Agate, a Lord and a pauper whose paths appear to diverge as time progresses, yet whose friendship seems to converge simultaneously. The fact is this: their paths, like the stars, are destined to cross. The question is this: what shall become of the stars upon collision?

THE MUTUAL SILENCE FOSTERED A QUIET UNDERSTANDING...

The cell was dark and dreary. He had been thrown in at night, with no light to guide him. He had assumed himself alone, considering the stark lack of a breath or voice. The cell even lacked the movement of a mouse or other pest. Ferre was one not want for company, though with the now rising sun he realized that he was not alone. A fellow his age or perhaps slightly younger sat slumped before him like the ward of a field. The boy's shallow face looked as carved gypsum, silent and unchanging like the proud statues of the mythical Rome. He was pale and poised like those statues too, with the impossible softness of marble, and moved just as much despite his waking eyes. Ferre was startled at the sight and held his breath.

The boy's paltry red lips crept into a small smile, as did his small, rounded eyes.

"Be not afraid," he said with a voice as soft as his white ringlet hair. When his head raised to face Ferre, his eyes could be properly seen. They were a storm of rings which varied in soft grays, pinks, and purples, bulls-eyed by rose-color pupils. They looked at Ferre, but one could tell at a glance that they could not fully see him. The irises danced around, shaking. "You should consider me a friend. It will be good to have a friend around here." He suspired, and at the same time Ferre released his own breath. The two sat meditatively upon a floor lined with stray stones.

Ferre turned his head towards the window as the other began stacking the pebbles on the side of his foot. He would misplace a stone, or perhaps it was too heavy, and the tower would balk and fall. Repeatedly, the boy would begin again, with the utmost care for his trifling. With a focused expression, Ferre picked at his cuticles until his nails were dark and bloodstained.

"I don't suppose you see new faces often." Ferre said, finally putting his fingers down. Another of the towers fell.

"I don't see faces much at all." He said impassively, yet still holding that same small smile.

"Forgive me."

Agate shifted, yet unmoved. "Had I been a debtor I'd be allowed to go out and meet as many friends as I'd like," in a stale tone.

"If not a debtor what may you be? Awaiting trial. What for?"

"We are kept in the same cell, good fellow. What are you awaiting trial for?" smirking.

Ferre once again sat silently, until his eyelids rose, his face drawn up by the hand of surprise.

"You may call me Agate. It shall be a pleasure to stay with you." said the other, extending his hand.

"Well met." Ferre said, looking to Agate's hand before his eyes returned to his own. With bloody fingertips he accepted the gesture.

Agate haled his hand to his lips but Ferre quickly pulled it back, as if burned by white flame.

"You are a young lord, are you not?" Agate said, taking no offense at the gesture.

"I am a dead man, soon enough."

"It may not yet be so. If you feel comfortable, I'm curious to hear the story of how a pecunius[1] one such as yourself was dragged to jail. It is strange to me that you are not kept in a castle-room instead. What might you have done to upset the jailer so?"

"Perhaps at another time." he said, diminished, and Agate did not pry. This jail was one unfamiliar to Ferre, but the atmosphere was not. Stone gripped by grime, solitary and cold. They were the same as the walls which made up his home.

The castle Hornblende was, most days of the year, empty. A hollow building with no soul, comparable to that of a solemn grotto. His father, Marquis of the march in which they lived, was tasked with directing the armies of the border during the great war. His father had also brought his older brother Magne along as an apprentice of sorts, to learn of war first-hand. For most of his days, Ferre waltzed idly through his liturgical lessons, chivalric teachings, and knight's training. He resisted bothering his elder brother for most of the day, for he was busy learning to be the next Marquis. As the second son it was expected that Ferre would join the church, though he cared not for such a career. It was far more likely that his father would appeal to the idea of him becoming a constable under his brother instead, considering his military mind. The fact that he had a younger sister who would soon grow into a well-mannered woman to be married off helped to support the notion that the family need not worry so about financial matters.

The greatest issue in his attempt to focus on becoming a constable was that his father had never been home to appeal to. The Great War had been especially taxing on the country's resources, and it had gone on many years before and following Ferre's birth. He could remember the day when they had lost. Better yet he could remember the day when his father had returned home.

---

[1] pecūniŏus adj.
wealthy, rich

It had been the midst of May. His father had arranged for a party to be held to welcome himself and his men home. After years of a quiet, numbing suffering in war, both those at home and those arriving were eager to lighten up with good food and drink.

Being one who did not favor noise and people, but was left to mind himself for the greater part of the year, Ferre found a conflict of joy and discomfort at the arrival of such celebrations. Though the night began pleasantly enough, consisting of pleasant mirth and melody, it devolved into a raucous heap of drunken splendor. The oft bitterly vacant castle's belly was filled with the fires of alcohol and flavor, cacophonous with the joyous cries of winedrunk men. Even the loam yonside its lichenous blue walls was lit far into the night by the roaring bonfires and those who stood round them. Ferre grew anxious as the air grew heavy with the breath of many; feeling similarly to dragging one's hand through thick velvet.

He was grateful for the food at least, and was able to dine on his favorite delicacy–pheasant graced with the flavor of caraway and encrusted with chopped almonds. He was allowed to sit at the table where his brother, father and his best knights and cavalrymen were arranged. He was shocked at the things his father was saying; it had been strange enough to hold a grand feast following his losses, but what he heard now could not be explained away.

"Now that he's lost us the war, we shall have his head!"

"He will be our majesty no longer."

"That shard-borne daffe shall get what he's been begging for this past decade."

Boorishly, his father and men were slandering the king. It was surreal, for the few times Ferre had been granted an audience with his father or his acquaintances, he had heard nothing but praise and waxed lyrical for their king. He realized now that perhaps his father's fulsomeness had been to appeal to his majesty, or anyone who happened to be connected and witnessed his actions. His father had been granted the title by the king's father, so aside from being his subject and loyal marshal he had no reason to feel the least bit indebted to him.

Now, he heard word of the king's failures. Drunkenly, his father cried, "His disservice shall be... remembered. To send so many willing young men to their deaths for a losing war is a crime against this country and a crime against God!"

"We had told him the effort was," Magne hiccuped, "hopeless many a time. It is his own fault for failing to hear the scream of a mountain's lion and... still wishing to per, persist."

Ferre was sheet-white and silent. He often did not contribute to the conversations of his seniors, only speaking when his father prodded him, but he dare not utter a word in this climate. He felt that he was standing in a field in the dark, and risked stepping on a hidden serpent dare he move further.

It was then, suddenly, Ferre had realized he had not truly known his father at all. In comparison to the knights which surrounded him he was more akin to a stranger than a son. They had been aloined for many years, and for the first ten or so Ferre had felt still a closeness with him. A symptom of his childish naivety working in marriage with his unrecognized lonesomeness. Yet, as he matured, during events such as this, he came to realize their disaffection. His father had never liked the king, he simply sought promotion. He wondered if his father's affections for him came simply from a sense of duty or goodwill.

"Excuse me, I'm afraid I must retire." he snuck the utterance between a break in the raucous conversation. The men laughed with great volume, but did not reply.

Feeling sick and longing for the more quieted naturesse of his mother, Ferre fled to the upper halls of the castle which was barred from the guests most many. Faltering for a moment to knissen[2] upon her door, Ferre gathered courage and entered the starkly quiet room following a light knal[3].

---

[2] cnyseð v.
to knock

[3] knal n.

"Mere[4] of mine, are you awake?" He whispered, seeing the room dark.

"How could I not wake, following the knal of my son?" She replied faintly. "Fear not, and do not ask forgiveness, for I have been awake for quite some time. 'Tis thanks to the shouts and hollers of your father and his company." she said, with a soft smile. At this point in time, she had been stronger, and even been with child–this would be Ferre's younger sister Alumine. She was enveloped by plush bedding and fine silks, as if laying in a bed of rich green hills with the most pleasant look upon her face. "Did you survive the barbarians?"

"I made a valiant effort, but in the end their forces were too great. I was forced to retreat." he joked.

"Sometimes our best is not enough, child." she whispered, bringing her hand to stroke his hair, which shone the color of soot and laid flat like her own. "Only the Lords know truly our struggles."

Suddenly, a great knal resounded from her door. A voice bellowed, "It is time for your liveneth[5]! Thank yer mother, wretch."

---

blow, knock
[4] mēre n.
mother
[5] lifnaðr n.
provisions, subsistence, victuals

Photo by Jonas Carlson

Front Street Writers Manistee
2023 Class

INSTRUCTOR INTRODUCTION: FRONT STREET WRITERS MANISTEE

Lauren K. Carlson

What you're about to read is compiled from creative writing classes held at Manistee's Armory Youth Project in partnership with NWS's Front Street Writers programming. Manistee—a town of 7,000 permanent residents and the historic homeland of the Little River Tribe of Ottawa Indians —is a lumber-boom town nestled between Manistee Lake and Lake Michigan. Factories line the shore of Manistee Lake, among them Morton Salt, Packaging Corporation of America and Martin Marietta Magnesia Chemicals.

Like most students in Michigan, the contributors to these pages experienced Covid shut downs and restrictions. The youngest, in grades six and seven, had the better half of their elementary years disrupted by the global pandemic.

Throughout their work, you'll find themes related to the passing of time and grief at uncontrollable changes. There is also a focus on coping, whether through exploring new activities or spending time with pets. Last, poems exploring identity, self and relationship to others, give voice to nurturing expression and confidence.

This is the context out of which these poems and essays were written. As their teacher, I was honored to nurture the creative voices of students in my town. It's with gratitude for NWS as an organization, all our friends, supporters and readers, we share this work.

TO WRITE
Lola Piper, 12th Grade

The truth is that
Words are not scary.
They don't come alive
To hurt you.
They do come alive,
But,
The words that fill pages
Aren't alive until you read them.
Words don't have meaning
Until you create it.

And that is the joy of writing.
It is the ability to make something
Out of nothing.
You are the God
And the paper is your world
And the pencil your tool.

You are cultivating expression.
Gardening the words
And growing ideas.

With words you are free.
The words bring endless
Amounts of liberty.
Because no one will stop you
From being who you want to be.

PANIC, STRESS, TALK
Grace Condon, 8th Grade

Meeting someone new.

Talking alone.

Walking, running, sprinting alone.

It's hard to talk.

Your mouth runs dry.

You don't know what to say, you're too shy.

It's scary, you're sweating you start to panic.

You're counting down to yourself 3, 2, 1.

But you don't have the guts to speak out loud,

only in your head so it's safe and sound.

But you must try.

You must speak.

You know you have to.

Even if nobody is listening.

It will only get more stressful if you keep it inside.

So speak your voice, it deserves to be heard.

SO I THOUGHT
Grace Condon, 8th Grade

      So I thought of the moon.
So I drew the moon.
      I thought of the stars
and I drew them.
      I thought of looking at space through glasses
and so I drew it.
      It was in my mind.
      So I put it on the page.

                —In mind
                      On page

THE VOICE
Thomas Racine, 6th Grade

Have you ever said hello?
I can't talk,
The truck is quieter than
my thoughts. I wish I had
hearing aids.

Have you ever made sound?
I didn't speak,
Vehicles are silent as air.
I need vibration helpers.

Question sound you have?
My body can't speak,
Cars are quieter than mine thought.
I need hear.

Quagmire vibrate?
Me no air shake.
Transport is no sound like thinks.
Help hearing I need.

Sound. H-E-L-L-O?
Can't air move?
Move machines no vibrate as think.
For hearing need I.

SCHOOL CLOCKS
Alexis McClellan, 8th Grade.

Why do people sit there with their
eyes on the clock all the time?
The teachers speak so loud,
their voices like fireworks.

How I wish the clock went
as fast as a cheetah.

SOMEDAY I'LL LOVE LOLA PIPER
lola piper, 12th Grade

you hate
you hate the way your smile raises higher to the right
than to the left and you hate
how thin your lips are
as they part into a grin.

hate
hate the way that when a stormcloud emerges
the rain never seems to stop,
and how you seem to drown in the pools it produces
and don't try to escape.
but some days the sky parts and they look down at you,
with his football jersey and her bright red hair,

and frown,
because you don't appreciate the life
they each never got to live.

lola,
you need to see –
see how the sun still shines on the darkest days.
that the smile you hate so much
is doing what they had taken from them.
so you should smile more,
and they will smile back at you.
someday you'll love lola piper.

REASONS WHY YOU ARE A GREAT MOTHER

Lola Piper, 12th Grade

The way that you take time off of work for me.
The times that you stayed home when I wasn't okay.
When you held me before I left the intake room.
The way you tell me everything will be okay,
when it most likely won't be at least for a while.
The times that you held me tight because I wasn't okay.
The times that you held me tight because you weren't okay.
The way that you hate white chocolate and moths.
The way that you always get me a gift for valentine's day.
The way that you hid the scissors, razors, and tweezers.
The fact that I know you will do anything for me to feel safe.
The no ends that come with your love.
The way that you always say you love me, even if we're fighting.

THINGS THAT ARE UNSAYABLE TO YOUR MOTHER

Lola Piper, 12th Grade

The reason you were at the beach until three in the morning.
Why the motion sensor flood light went off last night.
The train that you rode to three towns over.
The rundown Pizza Hut shed that you raided.
Leaving your phone in a bush and taking the bus downtown,
and plungers on the dollar store ceiling.

THIS IS NOT ABOUT A LABEL
Lola Piper, 12th Grade

For two years now I have been autistic.
For two years I have had the answers to my questions.
And for two years I have wondered
if anything has really changed.

Because three years ago
I still didn't like the beads in stuffed animals,
and four years ago I still had to lay on my left side to fall asleep,
and six years ago I still wouldn't tolerate the texture of egg whites,
and ten years ago I still went to bed at eight,
and fourteen years ago I was still fixated on cats,
and seventeen years ago I still hated being touched.

And so I wonder
if anything really changed with a label.
Because for 16 and a quarter years I was not autistic,
I was just Lola.
And it turns out a label
wasn't just an answer to my questions.

A label was a reason.
A reason to send around my private thoughts.
A reason to whisper behind my back,
although it was never really that quiet.
And a reason to use slurs that you should never say.

Because apparently two years ago,
something changed.

OLDER BUT NOT WISER
Leah McClellan, 8th Grade

Is growing up a good thing?
I can't see my elementary years,

I can't see the extended spring break.
What's the point of growing up?

My education is all I think of.
How I wish time could be a sidewalk.

Sidewalks aren't changed unless
they have to be.

THINGS I FOUND IN THE ABANDONED SCHOOL

Jacob Szynski, 6th Grade

I found a monitor smashed to pieces.
An old sign that said Mr. Edmundson's 4th Grade class.
There was something nasty (I can't say) on the floor.
I found a bunch of ribbons: First Place Track.
A medal left behind from the talent show in Detroit.

THE FIRST DIVE
Marlee Hamilton, 6th Grade

Diving may be
harsh, gets intense

while high up
on the board.

Taking a deep breath
and looking down,

then went down.
Felt like I
was diving off

a high building
or maybe a mountain

but when my hands
hit the deep
water

my mind feels
empty,

like my thoughts
fell in the

water with me.
Cheering and clapping

from my parents,
siblings, friends as

I get out
of the water

that I was
so scared of
before.

Feels so nice
To be on
my feet now

Just like my
First steps.

KINDERGARTEN LOVE
Marlee Hamilton, 6th Grade

When a boy on the
playground proposes in front of his
friends, you say yes because

that's the only thing you
can say in kindergarten.

2 hours later at the
second recess comes the wedding.
People surround around the hill

as a random boy you
don't know hugs you, and

puts a ring pop on
the wrong finger. People cheer
and you think it will

last forever. Have this 6
year old husband for your whole life.

Well, nothing lasts forever.

THE DAY I GOT MY DOG (IN 2 PARTS)
Leah Szynski, 6th Grade

Part 1: From My Perspective

One morning when I woke up, there was something very hyper and fluffy by my bedside. When I opened my eyes I saw a very fluffy black puppy. I have wanted a dog since I was 5. Even at a young age, I wanted a new friend to play with and now I finally have one.

Her name is Daisy and her breed is a aussie doodle (short for an Australian shepherd mixed with a golden doodle). When she calmed down I saw that she had a gray collar on with a bow on the side. As soon as I stood up the jumped and licked my face clean.

She was so impatient. I got dressed and went outside to play. We played in the yard with her squeaky ball and then my brother took her for a walk. This was the best puppy I could ask for. She is so nice and sweet for being less then a year old.

When it was night we played and ate dinner. She was tired by time we got done, so she fell asleep fast on my bed.

Part 2: My Dog's Perspective

One morning when I was sitting in my cage I saw a new person I have never saw before. He looked at me and looked at my owner at the time and said, [that's the one]. I was so confused and then all the sudden I was being let out of my cage and my owner handed my bucket of stuff to the random guy.

I was thinking [hey that's my stuff], but before I could even bark I was being lead to a big white truck. I was so confused but as soon as I knew it, I was getting into the truck. I was sad because I was leaving my owners. But as soon as I walked in this random house I saw a girl. A girl that seemed so happy to see me. I was over-filled with excitement and then she finally got up and I gave her hugs and kisses.

She even took the time to go outside with me. I was so happy playing with my favorite squeaky ball. Then a boy came out with a leash and took me for a nice long walk. When I returned to my new home I ate my puppy dinner and played. With my long day of excitement I was so tired so I crawled on the girl's bed and when to sleep.

EXPLORING
Jacob Szysnki, 6th Grade

One day me and my friend Jonas, we're going to look for abandoned buildings. And we find one, in the middle of nowhere. We went to explore it, and we found an abandoned gas pump and four shacks. A barn that had a tractor, fork lift. When all of the sudden I hear, click-clack, click-clack. I see an Amish buggy, so Jonas and I duck down. We let them pass by. After they pass by we went to explore the shacks.

I was stunned. In the first, so much stuff had been left in there. In the second shack there wasn't that much, but there was three old Pepsi bottles and a trap. I took the old Pepsi bottles and trap and gave the bottles to Jonas.

We went to the third shack. There was barely nothin' in there. So we went to the fourth shack and it was the same as the third. Me and Jonas went to the car to head home.

OLD MANISTEE HIGH SCHOOL
Jonas Carlson, 6th Grade

Introduction

Manistee High school or Old Manistee High school was built in 1927 it had 60,000 square feet, a gym, auditorium, 3 floors, and 30 classrooms. It was closed in 2004 and a new school was built.

Why was it shut down?

Well, first of all there was crumbling mortar and the structure was not very safe. During a bad rainstorm, little holes popped up everywhere in the roof. Over time it slowly it got worse and worse and worse. Eventually MAPS was not willing to pay for it, it was too far gone. So MAPS started a 30 million dollar bond, and started construction of a new high school for 33 million it included 130,000 square feet, and 30 classrooms, a gym and auditorium.

Abandoned Stage.

Before it was torn down it sat abandoned for 19 years. All the windows were boarded up. There was a school built next to it, Kennedy, that replaced the MHS into the junior high, or the middle school. The bridge that connected them was walled off and the elevator was unable to go to the 3rd floor. Most of the lead paint was peeling off. Ceiling tiles were falling off. The metal beams were rusting and the lights falling from the ceiling.

Tearing Down the Building.

In 2021 the vote was passed to tear down the school and build a new school and remodel the Kennedy building. A 30-million-dollar bond was started, and later in 2022 the tearing down of the building was started. Sometime around November, the building was finished being torn down. No work has started on the new building so far.

Future of MAPS

MAPS is planning to add a new building, remodel the Kennedy, and tear down Jefferson—a school from k-2. No work has started on the new school building or tearing down Jefferson, but some work has started on remodeling Kennedy.

Photo by Jonas Carlson

Front Street Writers Creative Writing Lab Grand Traverse
2022-2023 Class

INSTRUCTOR INTRODUCTION: FRONT STREET WRITERS CREATIVE WRITING LAB GRAND TRAVERSE

Kevin Fitton

The creative writing lab is a workshop-based class for high school students. Students do not receive school credit for taking this course, but we had eight students sign up for this class that met weekly from October through February. Each student wrote one piece of their own, while reading and responding to one another's work. I think it says a lot about the desire many high schoolers have to pursue creative writing that they're willing to put this level of time and attention toward an extracurricular class simply because they wanted to grow as writers.

This year we focused on three key areas of growth. First and foremost, we worked on the idea that writing is a process. It takes a lot to write a draft of a story or set of poems and then to share that with a group of readers. It's natural that culmination would feel like an endpoint. But it's not. Writing is a lot of hard work, and it's a process, so we worked on developing the mindset that a first draft is a starting point and not an end. This is a lesson that these young writers will have to keep relearning, as they move forward.

All of the students in this cohort wanted to focus on fiction, so we also worked on the key fictional components of character and setting. We looked at examples from Hemmingway, Alice Munro, and others, to better understand how great writers of fiction use these tools to tell their story. What's most exciting to me is that I saw my students growing in this area, and you'll see excellent examples of setting and character-building in these samples from our work.

It is always a joy to work with high school students who want to grow as creative writers. As a college professor, I have the opportunity to work with students at Western Michigan University,—and I've worked with adults as well—but I rarely see the level of talent and passion for writing that I see with a group of high schoolers when I teach with the National Writers Series.

FLOOD OF THE WHITE WALL
Sela Geraci, 12th grade

The White Wall was sturdy. It had been built with the founding of the city, built with the people's own hands and hearts, blood and sweat. It was what had kept the city from ruin, kept it from falling into turmoil and chaos. Kept it safe.

The stones were wide, thick stones from the dusty white mines of the mountains that were native only to this part of the world. The creases and cracks between stones had worn away, dirt filling them and the wind smoothing the upbearing stones, making the outside of the wall look almost seamless in its towering imposement.

The clouds above the wall were stormy, rolling promises of lightning and rain out to the world with light rumblings from the heavens. The world outside the wall laid flat and hazy with the drizzling of dark rain, and the White Wall stood like a faint lantern amid the growing storm. Water ran in rivulets down the wall, snaking from top to bottom, digging paths into the stone where the wind had blown away any others, pooling into pits of thick, sucking mud at the bottom.

Crowning the wall were dots of silver and brown, figures heavy with weapons and anticipation. Soldiers stood at attention, gripping their swords or bows, staring out into the hazy air, searching and standing and preparing. Each one stood with purpose, some with defiance and others with reserve, all ready for something to come. Their breathing filled the air, foggy breaths joining the rainy mist, water drops splattering against their armor of steel-plated leather with a light pattering. A faint buzzing of waiting weaved between the breathing and the rain, a feeling that was louder than any sound and thicker than the wall of mist that was growing out on the fields.

Walking among the soldiers, moving from one end to the wall the other and then back again, was a silver circlet that glinted brighter in the rain than the soldiers' armor. A simple circlet, only a remembrance of a crown, adorned the shaved head of the Captain, the city's leader and defender.

They met the eyes of each soldier, shared a nod or a comforting pat, a smile or a grimace, giving whatever each soldier needed from them to help each of them face the coming storms.

Lightning flashed in the distance, a growl of thunder accompanying it. The Captain glanced out onto the range of open dirt and grass, and the impending wall of mist. The rain had passed the point of drizzling and was now a heavy patter, coming down with force and the promise of worse.

The Captain laid their hand on the gilded hilt of their sword, a gesture of habit and comfort, as they stood in the center of the ranks of soldiers lining the walls and stared out into the mist, eyes roaming back and forth, searching.

"Captain" a man greeted, coming up to stand next to the Captain. His dark hair was plastered to his forehead, water falling off the layered plating on his shoulders in trickling waterfalls.

"Lieutenant," the Captain greeted, nodding their head. Their eyes never moved from the rain-and-mist filled field.

"Anything?"

"Nothing," the Captain answered. "It's this damn rain. It's taken away any visibility."

The Lieutenant only hummed. He ran his thumb along the string of the bow slung across his shoulder.

"We're ready," he said, confident. The Captain looked out along the wall, out along the lines of soldiers ready to fight. Each ready to brandish both weapon and might against whatever was waiting out in the mist.

"I know," the Captain said quietly, frowning and turning back to the fields of rain.

They stood there in the rain as the silence was slowly eaten up by cold and wet and waiting. The Captain's eyes never once strayed from the open fields though, their hand never loosening its grip on the sword hilt. A small frown grew steadily more grim on their face, water drumming down upon them, their eyes hard.

"What is it?" the Lieutenant asked, studying the Captain's face and their never-wavering gaze.

"What is what?" they asked.

"I know that look," the Lieutenant grunted. "Best tell me now rather than when we're bleeding out on the field."

This finally brought the Captain's gaze away from the opposing wall of rain and mist, if only to give a quick sharp glare to the Lieutenant. They sighed heavily, shoulders dipping.

"It doesn't feel right," they said, pursing their lips. "The rain... we never get fog banks this badly during this time of year, no matter how much it rains."

"It doesn't feel natural," the Lieutenant agreed. "They feel it too." He gestured to the lines of soldiers. "It's too cold and too heavy for the season. It's setting everyone on edge."

There was a pause.

"You don't think...?" the Lieutenant wondered tentatively.

"No," the Captain assured sharply, giving a quick shake of their head. "The Rose is secure, and no one should be aware of her capture yet. This is not her doing."

"Good." He nodded. "That's good." He didn't sound reassured, his lips pressed into a thin line.

The Captain shifted, adjusting their armor and circlet, droplets shaking to the ground.

"You know you could take that off," the Lieutenant said, gesturing to the silver circlet. "It'll only hinder you in a fight."

The Captain shook their head. "It is meant to show devotion to the fight, to represent duty. It will be lost in the war, I'm sure, but if we win then it will be found." The Captain paused and put a hand to their forehead, fingertips brushing the circlet. "Many things are lost in war. We can only hope that we'll find them again afterwards."

"You haven't lost your tendency for dramatics, I can see," the Lieutenant said wryly, smirking at the Captain.

"Nor you your sense of humor," the Captain responded, a hint of a smile on their Face.

"You like my jokes," he said, jabbing an elbow at them. "They're the only thing that brightens your day."

"You wish—"

A streak of lighting splayed out in the air, brilliant white sharpening the sky with jagged tendrils that brought dancing dots to the eyes of everyone. Thunder screamed through the air, shaking and rumbling through the ground and up the wall and making every soldier and stone tremble from sheer force. The wall shook and so did the soldiers' hearts.

And then, with a crackling inhale, the rain stopped. The heavy pouring quickly dried to a drizzle, and then nothing. The waiting that was buzzing through the air was eclipsed by something much bigger, something that whispered trepidation into the soldiers' ears on the rain-bereft wind.

"At attention!" the Captain yelled, gripping their sword hilt tight and straining their eyes through the thick fog. "Archers, ready!"

Bows were hurriedly pulled out, arrows notched with trembling fingers as the fog shifted forward and a rushing filled the air, a heavy sound of water echoing out from the fields.

"What is that?" the Lieutenant whispered, his arrow pulled back and scanning across the blocked horizon.

"I don't know," the Captain murmured, their hand raised and prepared to launch the first volley of arrows, fingers twitching. There was nothing to shoot at, no soldiers or troops, just an empty, soaked field and a building pressure within the wall of mist. The wall of fog was even closer now and creeping ever nearer to the White Wall, tendrils of cold mist trickling forward.

The roaring grew greater, a rushing from within the mist, louder and louder.

"Prepare yourselves!" the Captain shouted just before the first wave came, a huge crest of water pushing out from the fog and crashing down on the wall, sweeping soldiers out over the edge and falling back to the ground behind the wall. Screams carried over the mighty whispering of wave after wave of water shaking the White Wall's foundation.

"Hold steady!" the Captain shouted, useless against the sweeping tirade of waves.

The battlement on top of the wall filled with water and it tugged at the Captain's boots, trying to pull them down the other side of the wall. Screams filled the air and then were smothered just as quickly as water filled the lungs of those dragged under.

"Captain, this way!" the Lieutenant shouted, dragging the Captain away just as another huge crest hit the wall, shaking the stones to their core.

On the third wave, a figure stood upon the water, carried in by the sweeped waves and landing easily on top of the White Wall as soldiers continued to be drowned all around.

He looked around, eyes dark and cold, and the water parted at his feet, clearing a path and dragging away anyone who came near.

"It's the Tide," the Lieutenant whispered, horror in his voice.

"Lieutenant, go warn the people. Make your way to the Council if you can. Get as many people out as you can," the Captain ordered, gritting their teeth.

The Lieutenant squeezed the Captain's shoulder, knowing and sadness in his eyes.

The Captain gave their old friend a smile, a genuine one, and patted him on the back.

"The circlet won't be found this time," they said, quietly.

"Someone will find it," the Lieutenant said softly. "Someone will always be there to pick up the mantle."

Then he left, pushing through the dragging tides to get down the wall and to those sitting tight inside of the White Wall.

The Captain turned and made their way towards the Tide. the two locked eyes, cold clashing. A path cleared for the Captain. They walked forward, water clinging to their boots as their footsteps clapped against the wet stones. The Tide stood, watching the Captain.

The Captain stood in front of the Tide, and for a moment, they both just stared, gauging, waiting.

"You must be the Captain," the Tide said.

"And you must be the Tide," the Captain replied, frosty calm in their voice.

"You know who I am," the Tide said, a hint of surprise.

"I do." The Captain nodded.

"So you know why I'm here?"

The Captain nodded again. "I would request that you stop the flood if we are to talk," the Captain said, an edge of demand lacing their voice. The Tide grinned, dark and broad.

"I don't think there's a need to talk," he said, letting the water swirl threateningly around him. "I will be leaving with the Rose one way or another. You cannot stop me."

The Captain tilted their head. "Can't I?" they asked.

"I am ready to break down your precious wall in a matter of moments," the Tide growled, his grin dropping from his face and replaced with a snarl. "You are in no position to bargain."

"Perhaps not," the Captain agreed. "But I didn't think that you were in the practice of killing innocents."

"You mean like how your people have killed innocents?" the Tide growled. "How you've massacred my people until there's barely fifty of us? How you've razed our cities and our culture to barely anything, and shown no remorse or mercy? I don't think I need to be concerned about killing a few innocents when they are the same as those who have killed millions more."

"You're generalizing," the Captain responded smoothly. "The people behind this wall will be no different from yours: just people who were trying to live instead dead and buried beneath the actions of those with power."

The Tide scoffed. "You have no right to lecture me about this. You know nothing of the death of innocents."

The Captain stared hard at the Tide, their eyes stone cold. "We might not be the same," they said, "but we both know death. That I can assure you."

"And you will know of it even more if you do not return the Rose to me," the Tide said. Water lapped over the Captain's feet, soaking through their boots.

"So that you both can come back and drown us all with thorns in our lungs? That's not a choice that I can make," the Captain said, voice hard.

"Then you shall drown with water in your lungs instead."

The water rushed forward, grabbing the Captain's legs and pulling them over the ledge, roaring through their ears as the ground disappeared above their feet and they dropped down, choking back water, to the ground. The world swept around the Captain and things hit them in a muted clashing, rocks, sticks, people, everything coming towards them all at once and rushing away again. Everything was swirling and shifting in the water, wave after wave bearing down.

The Captain managed to push to the surface, lungs burning and begging for breath, only to get a mouthful of sea water and to be pulled under again. Something hit the Captain on the head, hard, and then there was no difference between the swirling darks of the water and the fading black stars in their vision. There were screams, gargled screams that melted into sea foam in the Captain's ears, mixing with the bubbling of water and a ringing deep in their skull.

The whole city was flooded, houses filled and sucked out by greedy waves, lungs filled with water that left no room for air, everything lost beneath an ocean of dark waters and darker hate. The White Wall crumbled, falling in pieces and chunks, large stones tumbling to the earth, meeting gravity for the first time in centuries. Dust filled the water, fine white mixing with dark blue. The city was swallowed, wall, people, and all.

The waves settled once all the screams choked off. Out of the sea-soaked ruins sprouted roses, bright white roses with vines of dark red spreading out from their centers.

The Tide walked among them, smiling heartachingly at the growing roses as he walked through the remains of the city, moving past crushed houses and bloated, bloodied bodies without a second glance. He stopped his meandering in front of the Captain's body, still shivering with the last desperate holds of life, streaks of blood melting into watery rivulets.

The Tide smiled sickeningly down at them and crouched, staring at their gasps with empty eyes. Their silver circlet sat soaked on their head and gleamed with water droplets in the cold sunlight peeking out from calming clouds.

A woman walked through the roses towards the Tide, her long dark red hair dry and haloed in the chilling light. The Tide looked up at her approach and smiled brightly, leaving the Captain and their dying gasps forgotten.

"Rose," he said, love pouring from his voice. He stood and went to her, wrapping her in his arms and tucking her against his chest, smoothing her hair and pressing kisses to her face. She gripped him tightly, pressing her face into his shoulder and breathing in and out measuredly. Slowly, she started shaking, sobbing into his shoulder. He pulled back and wiped tears gently from her cheeks, ducking down to catch her eyes. "Rose, Rose, what's wrong?" he asked.

She looked up, her brilliant green eyes meeting his, and brought her hands to his face, touching her fingertips to his cheeks. Her eyes were tear-filled, and Tide smiled sadly at her.

"I know," he said. "I know."

He didn't know.

From her fingertips, trickling black roots spread out, writhing with growth under his skin. He flinched back, but she grabbed onto his face and didn't let go, no matter how he tried to thrash away. Sobs tore from her throat as he cried out in pain, the dark roots growing thicker and thicker and spreading all over his body. Blood dotted his skin as green stalks sprouted from his flesh, white buds blushing red from his blood as they bloomed from his body.

"Rose," he screamed, shaking and dropping to his knees as he stared up into her green eyes, still streaming tears. She fell to her knees next to him. "Wh— why?"

"You killed them all," she said, pressing her forehead to his. "My love, you killed all of Them."

"Th— they deserved—"

"They deserved nothing," she said, quietly, the words murmured onto his skin as he continued to be the earth for blood-red roses. "They were only people. People just like ours."

He opened his mouth, but black roots tied around his tongue, blood trickling from the corner of his mouth. Petals grew from between his eyelids, thorns sprouting from his ears, his skin a bloody garden of roses. His breaths were gargled, blood dripping from his eyes and ears and fingertips, falling onto the ground. With a silent sob, she removed her shaking hands from his face, watching with quiet grief as he fell to the ground, choking on blood and rose petals.

"How could you do this?" she sobbed, whispering the words to an empty body.

The Rose folded in on herself, arms wrapped around her shaking body as she let her tears fall to the ground as quietly as she could manage. She cried and cried, letting her tears water the earth, eyes staring off into nothing as the body of the Tide laid lifeless on the ground before her.

As her tears dried, the shaking, shivering breaths of the Captain grew louder, the final desperate grasps for air. The Rose wiped her tears and walked over to the almost-lifeless body of the Captain, looking down upon them stonily for a moment before reaching down and brushing their hair from their eyes. With trembling fingers, the Captain grabbed her wrist and opened their trembling lips.

"Pick up... the ma—mantle," they said between shuddering, coughy breaths. Their other hand grabbed at the silver circlet upon their head, scratching at it and dragging it down their face. The Rose took it from them and placed it on their chest, listening with a face like a winter lake. "Protect... the people. All of... the people." The Captain coughed, watery heaves scraping at their throat. "No wall... unite... them..."

The Captain's fingers went loose over their grip on the circlet, their ragged breaths fading away into nothing. The Rose held their hand until the light left their eyes and their chest stopped moving.

Standing slowly, the Rose held the silver circlet almost reverently in her hands, watching as the water droplets fell to the ground from her shaking hands. Taking a deep, shuddering breath, she wrapped her fingers around the cold metal and grew a string of small rose buds around the silver, letting the roots and stems wrap around the still closed blossoms.

"I wish you all a peaceful rest," she whispered to the ruins. Looking out at the flooded city, the Rose gripped the silver circlet and smiled sadly through her tears at the destruction littered with wet bodies and bloody roses. "I hope..." she whispered, and placed the circlet upon her head.

EXCERPT FROM US
Delaney Cram, 12th grade

Our mother loves to tell the story. She didn't use to, I'm told. She used to shy from it, explain the situation in a tragic sort of way, only if we left her no choice. She used to think it was a little embarrassing, a little sad, to admit she had two children with just one body, but now she seems to find it wildly funny. Granted, she also drinks a lot more than she used to. That's Ona's aside though, not mine. I think our mother is glorious. After all, she didn't leave.

Why do you let your child wear that? Wait, what is your kid's name again? I thought it was Peter, but...

The questions come all the time, and they're not always polite. Mom doesn't have to explain, but I'm always glad that she does. I don't like to deal with it myself, but I'm glad she gives the complicated answer to *why?* since it is the truth and I like it better than the assumptions. It is one of the few things that Ona and I agree on.

In any case, when one of these well-intentioned (or more often enough, unabashedly curious) acquaintances of my mother's asks about me, about *us*, she will tilt her chin up a little and laugh in that way that shows off that off center tooth in the back of her mouth. She'll thrust one narrow hand into her hair, pulling long, thin fingers through thick, unruly curls, and say, *It's kind of an unbelievable story, actually. But, I swear to you, every bit of it is true...*

When my sister and I were born, only one of us was alive. Only one of my mother's babies was big and healthy and strong, only one of them started crying the moment their skin hit the sharp, sterile air, only one of them was facing any sort of life. The other one was shrunken and deformed, crumpled up and shriveled. The other one had skin that was sickly blue and puckered with chilled veins. The other one had no future beyond a little grave site and a murmured aside.

It happens a lot, with twins, my mother will say, a frown creasing the edges of her dark irises. She has golden rods in them that seem to glow in the right light, but dim just as readily when something upsets her. No matter how much she laughs about this, about us, I can never see those rods when she tells this story. *Sometimes there's just not enough nutrients for both of them and one of the babies will get more than the other. It's nobody's fault, but...*

She never finishes that sentence. I don't want her to ever finish that sentence.

My mother will continue the story. The doctor, she said, she knew from her church. And he was a very spiritual man. He liked her, she always said, rolling her eyes so that the white part smiled eerily through the crack of her eyelids. He asked her out once, before she met our father. He always had a soft spot for her, and that's probably why he did it.

The greedy baby and the dead baby were sitting on this cart and the doctor saw a little, shiny, misty thing floating up out of the dead baby's eye. Mom said that he was certain that it was the baby's soul. This part always seemed far-fetched to me. I've gone to church my whole life, but I don't think I'd be able to recognize a soul if I saw one, and I certainly wouldn't have done what this guy did next. But, what he did next, was grasp this little, disappearing soul in his fist and clasp his open palm over the living baby's eye. My mother said that this baby let out a shriek like Lucifer falling from Heaven or Icarus sizzling on the sun, and then both her children were in her arms and we've been like this ever since.

I'm not sure my mom's telling the truth. I'm not even fully convinced my sister and I do have separate souls. But, I like my mom's explanation, on the whole. Except for one part.

That baby that sucked the life out of its sibling? That baby that paid its penance for its selfishness in the womb by splitting the rest of its life in half?

That was me.

I wish I could say it's by the ocean, and salt gleams in the crevices of the disheveled base from where the tide lapped at its feet, an overzealous subordinate that thrives on its knees. Or maybe if it were tucked away in the deepest recluses of a forest, peering warily behind a willow's thin curtain and rooted firmly in the cool, forbidden earth, that would've been endearing. Even if it were perched stoically on a mountain, presiding over a forgotten kingdom, it might've been redeemable. But no. Nothing can ever be so enchanting, and be allowed to remain.

Our Castle stands at the base of a hill, at the edge of an empty lot that used to be a gas station. She is far from a castle, really. Made from rotted wood planks, chipped and crumbling bricks and concrete blocks, and bits of cardboard and styrofoam, among other pieces of junk we had managed to salvage over the years. She is decrepit, disheveled, and dangerous. I think she is the easiest thing I have ever loved.

Ona and I didn't build Our Castle. I mean, I guess we did, there's never not a *we*. But, she was mostly along for the ride. I built this with James, when we were eleven. James is my Marissa, I suppose. But that comparison feels like licking a cat from its tail to its shoulder blades, so I ought to stop there.

After I abandoned Marissa, I came here. To Our Castle. We hadn't been all that far, but I had run there, and my ill-equipped lungs flailed savagely about, thrusting against my ribcage and twisting around each other, snapping viciously at each breath I took like Roosevelt's piranhas. My heart had been shunted aside, pattering wildly from where it had been wedged somewhere below my clavicle, and I had one hand to that approximate part of my chest as though I could somehow soothe the rambunctious organ whilst my other hand braced against my knee, laboriously studying the faded concrete while I painfully remembered why I never stuck with track. Or baseball. Or soccer. God, I hate my anatomy.

You're so dramatic, Ona chided. *We're not dying.*

I was incapable of speaking or even thinking anything directly back to her, but she was well aware that I blamed my inability to regulate my breathing for why I could never play any of the sports I wanted to, and I blamed my inhibitions on her. It happens often enough with any of our motor functions. Two people with nearly equal control of arms and legs, eyes and mouth, and we're inescapably subservient to the other's any impulse. Seemingly random spasms in our limbs can be off-putting to strangers, but it's not debilitating. But, when suddenly someone else is breathing for you, someone else is inflating your lungs and contracting your throat, it is only understandable that some panic may ensue.

She doesn't mean to, I know that. They're communal lungs and neither of us has any more right to them. I'll still fight her on every breath she takes for me, though.

"Alright there, Peter?"

My head snapped up, neck as crisp and taut as a parachute cord. My gaze locked on the boy leaning against Our Castle, arms crossed and auburn fringe hanging just at the edges of his eyes. He was taller than I was, though by a mere half an inch, and he was much paler than me, freckles all up his arms and neck and face that made him look like a smallpox victim in this light.

This was my James.

I straightened, running a hand down my hair, breathing easier at the feel of each strand sighing against my palm. My heart stuttered as I strode toward him. *Cut it out*, I told Ona.

You know I can't control that, she thought with an eye roll so audible that I could almost feel my own eyes strain with the motion. It was so visceral that I wasn't entirely sure she hadn't just rolled our eyes, and my fingers instantly went to my eyelids, rubbing away the violation.

I'm not proud of how I treat her, like a nuisance, like some possessive creature from a horror film. But, God, how else am I supposed to react when my body, *my* body, starts moving all on its own?

"I didn't think you were coming today," James said, uncrossing his arms as he rummaged through his pocket.

I opened my mouth, ready to force some shallow laugh about Marissa driving me up a wall. But, as I was gathering air, my lungs suddenly felt like arms that were so weak and sore, and they just fell open, spilling all of the breath they had been collecting in one rough exhale. "I lost myself," I said shallowly. "I-I don't know where I went. Again."

He stiffened, slipping his hand out of his pocket and bracing it against Our Castle, as though ready to launch off of it. Then, his shoulders dropped and his back jutted against Our Castle, the collapse of his body creating two hushed taps, a hollow knock on a rotted tree. "Shit," he said finally. He reached back into his pocket, retrieving a thin, half-worn cigarette, and tucked it into his mouth. "Need one?" he asked, fiddling with his lighter.

He always asks, even though I always have to say no. Ona wouldn't stand for it.

And there it is, that slippery, greasy, throat-clenching thought. I always try to suppress it, as though that could ever work, as though thoughts can be retracted and forgotten, as though they could ever be anything private. *I wouldn't say no if my body were my own.*

Ona used to recoil from this as though I had offered her a searing fire poker and forced her to clasp it against her palms. She used to make my stomach roil and my brows furrow and my eyes burn and my hands curl into gnarled claws. Except that it was actually *her* stomach and brows and eyes and hands, which only hardens the initial line of offense.

In any case, she doesn't react anymore. At least not in any way that anyone else can see.

James pulled the cigarette from his lips the way my mother does, hanging lightly off the crook of the middle and index fingers, wobbling on its own little axis. Smoke streamed from the purse of his lips and hung over us for several seconds, for several decades as we stood there, watching a plastic cup of unknown origin roll over the faintest remembrances of parking lines.

"Maybe it's supposed to be like that," he said eventually, running the edge of his thumb along the cigarette's dry, crackling side. "Like, maybe you're supposed to take turns. I mean, Ona goes away sometimes too, don't you, Ona?"

"Yes," she said. Her voice was higher than mine, clipped and precise. "When no one's acknowledging me and I start to feel, I don't know, not involved, then I'll go away and do something else."

"Daydreaming," I nodded, snatching our larynx the instant her last syllable slid off our tongue. "But this isn't that. I don't remember anything after you got to Marissa's. I just...disappeared."

"Maybe you were daydreaming, and you just forgot what it was you were daydreaming about. I forget what I was thinking about all the time." James grinned, briefly flashing the tips of his thick front teeth. Ona was thinking something unsettling about how James's eyes were still narrowed and one corner of his mouth was clearly closer to his earlobe than the other corner, but I determinedly ignored her because I didn't want to think about James being unsure. James was never worried, even when we found a broken bottle in Our Castle that neither of us had put there or when Ona panicked and shot through a red light while he was teaching us how to drive or when his mother disappeared for three days with his five year old brother and a bottle of Percocet. If James was worried, then there was no hope for me.

"I think you're right," my voice said. It sounded like me, but it was Ona who said it. It's not the first time she's spoken for me. But James could usually tell. I glanced over at him, and he dropped the cigarette on the ground, smashing it under his ragged shoe. He brushed his palm along the top of his hair, so it stuck out the side of his head like horns.

"I saved the crossword this morning," he said, flashing his teeth again. "You want to try to solve it with me?"

I smiled back, briefly touching the tips of my fingers to a curl that had fallen out of alignment, pulling it taut behind my ear. "Yeah, sure," I said.

"But, you can't cheat," he warned, shaking his finger and eyes crinkling. "I know Ona's smarter than both of us."

My heart hammered again. What the hell? *What's the matter with you?* I asked, but her thoughts were too muddled and I didn't feel like dwelling on it anyway.

James shunted the slab of wood aside, entering Our Castle and I followed after him. It was dim inside, no windows but light nonetheless prickling in from seams in the walls and ceiling. Splintering boards hung over our head, with a heavy blue tarp over them to keep out the dew and rain. It was held in place by four cinder blocks, three of them broken in halves.

Covering the ground were sleeping bags and scraggly blankets and pillows that smelled like mildew. I'm not actually sure what mildew is meant to smell like, but I suspect it's something damp and tangy and akin to the sticky sourness of a rotten fruit's rancid juice dribbling down one's chin, slimy flesh cradling one's teeth.

I collapsed onto two of these pillows, taking care not to disturb the two thin rods stuck in an upside-down V in the middle of the room. James fell next to me, his head resting against a wedge of styrofoam, as he shifted the lumpy sleeping bag around beneath him. I pushed my fingers into a hole in my pillow's corner, past the bristling cotton to the pillow's soft inner cheek. I rubbed circles in it while James folded the newspaper over and trailed his pencil stub along the lines of the first clue. "A French woman author," he murmured. He whistled, flipping the pencil around and around in his left hand. He smelled like tobacco and chives. "You know any French women authors?" he asked, nudging my shoulder blade.

I shook my head. "I don't even know any French sounding names. Maybe 'Bonjour?'" "Hello?" Ona smirked.

"Why are you still here?" Ona used to fade away whenever I was with James. Not quite like how I left, of course, but she never used to loiter around us like this. Lately, though, she had been sticking around more and more. It was particularly annoying since James was much more tolerant of her than Marissa had ever been to me. Could anything ever be just mine?

"Bonjour's enough letters," James nodded. "But maybe we skip this one?"

"Try Colette," Ona said. Well, at least she was using her own voice inflections.

"No, that's too many letters," James said, tapping at the little boxes.

"No, it's not," I said, catching onto her thoughts. I reached over and counted out the letters as I touched each box. "C-O-L-E-T-T-E. That's seven."

"How do you know that?" James asked, filling in the name. "Our mother had a book of hers, I guess," I said.

"It was *Gigi* and she still has it. It's on the shelf in the living room."

James rocked a little, hitting his shoulder against mine. "Didn't I say Ona's too smart for us? If she keeps this up, we'll have to be done in like twenty minutes."

And then, something happened when I looked up at him. Like a hummingbird whirring in that artery in my neck, like a cat curling up and purring next to my heart, like rubbing a peach's untorn flesh against my parted lips. For the briefest of moments I felt dizzy and sick and awkward and *happy*. My heart had tripped over its feet again and I knew it wasn't Ona's fault this time.

He is cute, isn't he? Ona thought, a tentative, delirious whisper.

Oh. *Oh.*

Oh no.

ROARING AUGUST
Tess Tarchak-Hiss, 9th grade

A night in the warm muck of a midwestern August is the worst time to be alive. This is especially the case when the walls of my little room seem to be closing in on itself. The friends I had in school years previously vanished into thin air. My "friends" don't call in the summer. The phone line seems to go mute now, my house certainly does not. I don't even leave my 7x10 space in the summer, but I can hear every sound that happens in this house. The floorboards squeaking with every gust of air that passes through the cracks, and the mice who live in the cupboard next to the fridge squeeze out of their home to check out their familiar surroundings. Quiet things, usually.

Recently, not so much. Now I hear the slamming of doors in faces, screams ringing through the house, arguments flooding every room, instantly drowning and killing any smiles and warmth this house used to hold. It wouldn't even be like this if my dad didn't move back, and he hasn't even been here for a full day. I haven't seen him in at least a year, not since he smacked Mama across her face with a frying pan.

About a year ago, my sister, Diedre, was silently sitting on the nappy rug next to the stained coffee table. She was playing with a Smokey Bear stuffed animal, given to her by Mr. Gillespie down the street, as a thanks for her helping him tend to his small, overgrown garden. Dad was drinking his beer and smoking his cigarette, going on his usual nightly rant of how he could have been touring the country with his bluegrass band right now, but no record label could "understand their potential and talent." I was half-listening, but mostly watching my mother nearby on the phone, swinging her red curls back with laughter, her cheeks pink, eyes black and glossy. She was standing near the stovetop, heating oil in a pan for some mediocre meal. Dad never liked the way Mama's voice scratched when she talked on the phone, how she cackled at Mr. Gillespie's witty remarks when he would call her every night. He would scream at her to hang up, slam his guitar-playing hands on the table, and yank the phone line out of the wall. But this time, it was different. His intensity was higher than normal. I could see his veins pop out of his neck, his fists clenching. But she kept smiling and laughing, her slightly yellow-tinted teeth trapped inside a defiant smile. So he shut her up the only way he could: by grabbing the pan off the stove and slamming it across her face.

I watched her cheek hit the floor, the blood a dirty maroon liquid leaking like a burst pipe on the chartreuse rug. I wasn't sure what to do, and desperately looked towards Diedre for help, even though she was 4 years younger than me. She was frozen in shock, eyes fixating on the stovetop that my dad grabbed the pan from, the gas ring underneath it still lit. She let out a scream that shook the walls around us. My father stared at the two of us, a guilty look plastered across his face. However, it was more like the face of getting caught, if anything.

He ran to his truck, and screeched his way out of our driveway, as Diedre's tears fell down her face. I rushed to Mama's side, seeing what I could possibly do, but she was fully knocked out. I screamed at Diedre to help, and to run down the street to tell someone what had happened. But it was like she was frozen in time. Eventually help came, and mom stayed in the hospital for 7 months. Mr. Gillespie would occasionally help watch us, and give us pitiful looks. But Dad didn't come back. Not for 2 years, until this hot, summer night in August.

I've never really liked Diedre that much. She didn't do anything marvelous, but always seemed to be the center of everyone's solar system. Even so, I wanted her luscious ginger curls and big brown eyes, the same ones that she shared with my mother, instead of the mousy, lightish hair and gray eyes I got from my father. More than anything, I wanted the way my mother actually loved her. As much as she possibly could, at least. I was the "tryout kid", my Mama used to say. She had me at 15 when my dad was 18. Like my dad, she'd complain in her frequent drunken fits about how far she could have gotten in life if she didn't make dumb decisions at a young age, and how golden her life would been if she weren't stuck with the guy who got her pregnant.

I've lived with my sister for all 9 years of her life, and I still didn't know her that well. She was always quiet but stopped talking the day Dad left. Her silence was obnoxious though, defiant. At school, she was mute too. Someone would ask her a question and she would just stare ahead, blankly ignoring them.

She wasn't always speechless. She used to blabble constantly about national parks. Specifically the Indiana Dunes National Park, less than an hour away. She would beg my mother to drive us down, how she desperately wanted to see the towering dunes fall over each other. Mama ignored her until she just gave up.

Diedre just sits in the living room now, staring off into the cracked wall behind the stovetop and playing with her stupid little stuffed bear, in her own invisible enclosure. Each person in my house, including me, lived in our own little bubbles. We didn't dare overstep into the other's realm or break out of our own sphere. Growing up, I didn't learn how to love, especially not myself. So if I don't set my heart on anything or anyone, I never get disappointed. I'm 14, so I suppose I don't need to know what I want quite yet. I've never really thought of a world outside this wood-paneled house on Pier Street. All I've really thought about is running far away, from my mother and my father, from my sister, from those mice that live in the cabinet. I want to see what I'm missing out on in the world while I'm stuck here. I just want to be on my own, without the thought of another person floating around in my head.

•

Mornings are the only time I can hear the small sounds in the house, so I always wake up at 6 before everyone else does. I close my eyes and open my ears, and let the waves of sound pass through.

But at night, everything is up. Everything is loud.

On this night, I heard a loud slam, followed by a series of high-pitched screams.

"Where do you think you're going? You have nowhere to go, you don't have a job," I heard a familiar voice screech from the sofa. A voice I haven't heard in years. It took me a few moments to process what was happening. But sure enough, it was my dad. He must have come back last night.

"I'm heading out, Dom. And for the record, I do have a job. I got one after you almost, you know, killed me? And you left me here, alone, because you got scared and ran away? Like you always do. I had to support myself. I have nothing now, thanks to you," my mom snapped.

I heard his fist pound on the coffee table yet again. "I didn't run away Melanie," he tried to say, but Mama cut him off.

"Right. You were being a drunk douche, and your actions ended you up in jail for 15 months. You haven't even been here 24 hours, and you're already dragging this whole household down with you!" She screamed.

"This house has been a garbage dump since day one, Melanie, and you know that. The paint is chipping off the walls, you don't even have a washing machine. Instead of taking care of the house, and these freak kids, you've been at Gillespie's! And that's where you're going right now, isn't it?"

There was a pause, but I knew what Mama was gonna say. "David Gillespie moved to Michigan. His mother died. I haven't seen him since last year. And you know what? I would be with him right now if you didn't come along, and if these kids didn't come along, and if the world wasn't falling to shambles." She sighed, and I could hear her foot tapping against the wood floor. "Dom, you're a horrible person. But I'm done fighting for right now. I'm too tired. I want you out of here by the time I come back tonight. I want you to take all your shit and leave, and never come back." The door slammed, and I could hear the car putter down the driveway

I got out of bed and my dad was sitting on the couch, his hands covering his face. I looked at him in disbelief. Why would he come back? Why does he need to be here right now? I wanted to say something nasty but didn't have the energy. Diedre, who had been sitting through all of this, was sitting on the rug, hugging her Smokey Bear toy, and staring at the stovetop.

I looked inside the fridge, unsurprisingly not seeing anything but beer cans lining the inside. My dad stretched and stood up. "Diedre, what am I supposed to do? Huh? I have nowhere to go, this is the last place I can go. I have no friends, I have no real family. What am I supposed to do?" No response from Diedre, her gaze and attention was focused on something out of the blue

"Jesus, Diedre, look at me. Jesus." Unsurprisingly, no response. Just a deadpan look. "What is wrong with you? Speak! Speak!!" In a fit of rage, my dad took Diedre's Smokey Bear, lit the stovetop, and placed him on top of the burner. Dieidre's eyes were filled with concern and worry as Smokey's hat caught a flame. She leaped towards the stove, but not before my dad chucked the bear out of the window, in the nearby trash. My sister ran over, and my father slamming the window down before she could reach it. He lit a cigarette, leaving the matchbox on the stool next to his guitar in the living room, and went to his room.

Diedre instantly ran towards the trash, with the intention of saving the bear. Not knowing what to do, I looked awkwardly out the window. I wanted to reach out to Diedre, but I didn't know what to say. She came inside with a huff, made eye contact with me, and suddenly got up and grabbed the matches.

"Diedre, stop," I said, but she ignored me. She threw the match into the guitar, eyes filled with emotion and tears. The living room was filled with the scent of burning wood. "Okay, that's enough. I'm sorry about your bear I guess, but," I tried to say, attempting to stop her, but it didn't work. She lit match after match, throwing the small sticks of flame into my dad's most prized possession, and watching it disintegrate into the ground.

My dad must have gotten a whiff of the intense smell because he came rushing out. His jaw dropped to the floor, and he fell to his knees in front of his beloved instrument. Diedre dropped the matches, and stepped back, slowly and carefully.

"What the hell did you do?!" He roared. He ran to the sink and poured several glasses of water over the cello, watching the smoke rise to the top of the ceiling. He stood up slowly and faced Diedre, fire in his eyes. His veins were popping out, fist clenched, sweat dripping from his forehead.

"What the hell is wrong with you Diedre? You're a freak! An accident!" It seemed like Dad was at a loss of words until he pointed toward me. "Or did you do this? Did you stop her? Did you do it together?"

I looked down and shook my head. "No. I didn't stop her." Diedre was eventually still backing away slowly, and when my dad turned around to mourn over his 25-year-old guitar, she bolted out the door. Dad didn't even care. He sat by his instrument, stroking the pegbox and the bridge. Before he could say anything to me, I rushed to my room, locked my door, and covered my face yet again with the snowflake pillow.

I wanted to be a good sister to her because, in some way, I felt bad for her. I wanted to reach out to her, but I never knew what to say. I had no clue what she was feeling, I barely even knew what I was ever feeling. Every time I saw her on the mucky rug, staring into the cracks in the walls, I wanted to ask her, "What's wrong? Why are you the way you are? Why did you give up" I just had no idea what to do. I thought about it a little more and decided to go outside into the yard. I went out and saw her, lying near the trash. Her smokey doll was slightly charred from being cooked in the garbage. I took her hand and led her into the house, a matchbox in my pocket. We locked eyes, and I lit the first match. I handed her the box, and she lit the second. We threw the matches on the guitar and watched the fire rise and rise. She walked out of the house, matches in hand, and I followed her. Match after match we lit, before soon the whole wooden house was on fire. We watched and watched, the fire seemed to make the purple night sky turn warm shades of orange and red. As the flame rose to the top of the sky, I looked at my sister. She looked back, and a smile came across her face.

"Wanna go to Indiana Dunes?" I asked.

"That would be awesome." She responded.

Photo by Jonas Carlson

Writers Studio
2022-2023 Class

INSTRUCTOR INTRODUCTION: WRITERS STUDIO

Teresa Scollen

The Writers Studio program at Northwest Ed Career Tech offers a creative home and college credit for high school juniors and seniors. This is an intensive two-year creative, professional, and journalistic writing program built for students who love to write. We cover many creative and professional genres—poetry, nonfiction, playwriting, fiction, journalism, professional writing—and audio production in a collaborative, workshop-based environment. We build skills and then apply them to real-world situations. Students develop a writing portfolio, submit work to competitions, and seek publishing opportunities. Seniors may be eligible to work in an internship. Visits by published authors and other working professionals help students build a sense of the wider professional world.

Many students come into the Writers Studio with a real love of fantasy fiction, but not much exposure to other genres. One of our goals is to open up a wider sense of the varied world of writing. The pieces you see here were written during the fall semester, in brand-new genres: poetry, creative nonfiction, and playwriting. We really loved the discovery of and experimenting in new forms; we hope you enjoy reading this work.

THE JOY OF BEING HIDDEN
Minnie Bardenhagen, 11th grade

I detested the idea of returning the hoodie. In fact, I held onto it for several weeks after the fallout between me and my ex-lover. I couldn't bring myself to put it on, but I couldn't let go of it. Both would cause too much pain. That hoodie had my sweat and tears embedded into the fabric. It had heard all of my rants, my laughs, my shouts, and my careless actions. Throughout the days that he had made me feel weaker, powerless, it protected me. I was safely hidden within the hoodie.

It would be difficult to imagine a cozier day. The fire in the fireplace crackled and illuminated the small room. The clouds fountained snowflakes that blew with the wind. We watched them through the window while snug under blankets. That was the day my significant other gifted me with the Aeropostale hoodie. The inside was soft and hung loosely over my body. One of its dark blue sleeves had been torn slightly at the end, leaving a hole just big enough to poke my thumb through. The bold yellow letters running across the chest area contrasted with the dull grays and blues. The brand's name formed a rainbow over the "NO 87" placed in the top-left corner. On the untorn sleeve, "EST 1987" was printed.

The first appearance of a hooded sweatshirt was in the 1930s, when Champion Products allegedly created the item of clothing to aid athletes and laborers in harsh weather. Interestingly, this simple, practical idea later took on a significant new meaning. In the late 20th century, the hoodie was a convenient tool for lawbreakers who wanted to keep their faces unseen. This gained it a new reputation, one that sparked fear and suspicion.

The hoodie is a common sight nowadays. It managed to gain popularity among the general public in the 90s and early 2000s. However, this failed to eliminate any preconceived notions regarding hoodie wearers, especially if the wearer wasn't white. In Sanford, Florida during 2012, the world watched as injustice occurred. Trayvon Martin, a 17-year-old boy, was shot and killed by George Zimmerman, a neighborhood watchman.

Zimmerman described Martin as suspicious looking. That day, Martin wore a dark gray hoodie. Suddenly, an issue that had been hiding behind the curtains was thrusted into the spotlight. The hoodie became the face of a fight for racial equality and disposing of stereotypes in America.

It's frightening how for some, clothing becomes enough to kill. The way we assume so much about people so quickly disturbs me. Do I judge others so instantly? Do people judge me so instantly? Yes. People begin to judge each other at the first glance. Assumptions are normal, but more times than not, inaccurate. Acting on these assumptions can be dangerous, as the tragic story of Trayvon Martin demonstrates. Clothing is nowhere near enough to define who someone is, or what their intentions may be.

I wonder how people viewed me in that hoodie. Did they see the way I sat and stood with more confidence? Did they see my reluctance to speak up fly away? I could lean up against a wall with one foot kicked up and stare down the people who pass by without feeling like an idiot. I could strike a pose and act silly without wondering if I looked stupid. No one could see me under there. It's harder for people to judge something when there's nothing available to judge. The hair under the hood, the chest under the fabric, the arms under the sleeves – it was all put away. I was a mystery within those fabric walls.

I noticed how my lover's behavior would change, too. I could see him act cooler when surrounded by strangers. Being in a crowded room isn't so bad when you have a coat of armor. He walked with his trauma hidden deep in those pockets. No one could spot it, even if they tried. He and I were the age where all we wanted was to hide ourselves. We teenagers strive to cocoon ourselves in our clothing. Oversized clothing has the power to make our chafed thighs and our hip dips disappear. No longer do we have to cross our arms to hide our breasts and buckle our belts too tight for our stomachs. We feel more comfortable in our own skin by not showing our skin. Clothing that covers us makes us feel like we can express ourselves with less judgment. Our movements become less awkward. Our approach to social situations becomes more relaxed.

The night he gave me the Aeropostale, we hopped in his dad's large black GMC and traveled to the local theater. The sidewalks of Suttons Bay typically aren't frequented by many during the winter; therefore, it was the ideal time to enjoy everything the small town had to offer. The cuffs of the hoodie hung just below my fingertips. The cold winter air barely seeped through the fabric and into my skin. I wanted to catch the snowflakes flying past the beaming streetlights. The whispering wind blew the oversized fabric with it. My partner, who always had a hard time knowing his own strength, tapped my shoulder with what would have been enough force to cause a brief moment of pain. This was a regular occurrence, but this time it was different. The thick fabric covering me numbed the touch. Suddenly, I was invincible.

We walked down the carpeted isles of the 70-year-old theater, then sat on the aged cushions. I put my feet flat on the edge of the seat and pulled my knees into the hoodie. The hood rested on top of my head. My body heat bounced off the rest of the hoodie and made me my own heater. The theater wasn't even close to packed, but it wasn't empty. There were enough people so that it wasn't awkwardly silent, enough room to avoid feeling claustrophobic. Suddenly, I felt the static in my hair as the hood fell off. I put the hood back on and pulled the drawstrings tighter. Enclosing myself in the cotton eased any uncomfortable feelings.

The lion stalks its prey. Lurking behind the grass that grows high within the plains, it spots a lonely antelope, a perfect candidate for a potential next meal. Compared to the antelope, the lion is greater in size, sharper in teeth, and has a taste for meat. The antelope is grazing on its ignorant bliss, vulnerable to an attack, unaware that its future may take place in the lion's stomach. The lion slowly inches forward, getting ready to pounce. However, despite the apparent advantages of the lion, the antelope has the ability to escape the situation. Antelopes are creatures with copious stamina. That along with the horns on their head protects them from their enemies. Depression was a lion, watching me from the shadows, salivating, waiting for the right time to sink its teeth into my throat. The hoodie increased my stamina. The fabric was my horns. I could fend off the lion. I couldn't be preyed upon. I was safe.

According to a study reported on by Good Therapy, 96% of the 100 women interviewed believed that their confidence is altered by their clothing. That same study showed that women who are depressed are more inclined to wear clothing a couple sizes too big. Now, let's look at the current statistics on depression. Teenage girls are almost three times more likely than teenage boys to go through depression, according to Pew Research Center. They also conducted a survey that concluded that seven in ten teens had expressed that anxiety and depression was an issue in their community.

Based on the data, the link between clothing and mood seems to be plausible. Oversized clothing has been the big thing, and that might not just simply be the recurrence of a trend. We live in a world of broken brains. We have endured the pandemic. We have endured the dangers of social media. We have endured long standing issues such as unrealistic body standards. We were born into a world where racism and sexism were ingrained into our society, both blatantly and so microscopic that we don't pick up on it until it's too late. Our flaws are one of our greatest concerns, so to be able to hide those definitely helps ease the piles of pain the world has dropped on us.

I could see it when I walked into classrooms, and saw fields of baggy sweats and t-shirts down to people's knees. I joined the crowd seamlessly. We were all clones. I walked into gatherings with the socially gifted with more ease than before in the Aeropostale. Getting invited to the gatherings the girls liked to call "shindigs" was one thing, but feeling comfortable enough to open my mouth was something I never would've thought was possible for myself. We chowed down on pizza rolls and trash talked anyone who wasn't worthy of the girls' acceptance. It all seemed to happen with such ease, as if the hoodie deflected the opinions of others. There was this shared feeling of safety among us, like nothing mattered right now. No one could touch me with that hoodie on. It was exhilarating. For once

I wasn't holed up in my room bathing myself in my own tears, and instead I found myself laughing along with the wonderfully wrong crowd.

Some good things, unfortunately, can't last forever. The summertime heat began to melt away the connection that me and my lover thought we had. Problems didn't just begin to emerge – they had been present throughout the relationship, and it took a couple long talks with friends to see the reality of our situation. I had trusted him enough to tell him where I was the weakest, and that's where he always hit me. He would use my empathy as a weapon against me. It didn't matter how horrible he treated me, I always excused it because I knew I he had a hard life. Excuses were spat out for every time he made me shed tears and even blood. Depression began to weigh me down, and in my state of sadness, I found the answers blooming like the flowers. Shining bright on me like the rays of the sun. Buzzing around my ears like the bees. It would be difficult, but it was time to let go.

Letting go did mean letting go of the hoodie, which I (reluctantly) ended up returning. I scoured the men's section at Target for a replacement. I had grown accustomed to having that hoodie sitting there on my dresser, waiting for me to come home and put it on. It became a necessity rather than a want. Like water and food keep the body from withering away, my hoodie kept my body at ease. It was an extra layer of protection from those anxious knots in the stomach, those massive headaches after crying for hours. After a while, a soft, burgundy miracle appeared before my eyes. The lion was no match for me now.

EGO EGO
Sydney Boettcher, 11th grade

We all have our pride. It is as universal and insidious as a shadow, as invasive and all-consuming as the dark. It follows underfoot and waits patiently for a moment to strike, like a prowling housecat. Waiting for you to lose your balance. Your guard will eventually slip, and you will trip over it from time to time; for some people, it is all they do. Wandering around, so trapped in their own head they can't tell in from out. The modern tragedy is one of Ego. The lost bankers & children & politicians of the world, their facade of humanity cracking under the sheer weight of personality. Gooey chunks of purple Ego leaking out. The texture of silk and turpentine. They can fool themselves, and they can fool each other, but may they not fool you, or you will crack as well.

It is the ultimate motivator. Screaming in your head to show all those who would dare to mock you how much better than them you think you are. Ego drives people to be bigger. It is not the healthiest motivator, far from it. Listen too much and you will lose yourself, striving for forbidden perfection. Unattainable or not, Ego makes you think you are the exception. And you will spiral down into the fiery crash of burnout, the toll of working towards the impossible. Ego can go the other way, too. Instead of building yourself up, if Ego determines that to be too much work, it will tear others down. You can still be bigger than everyone else, with the added benefit of not having to do much of anything. Simply sabotage, sabotage, sabotage, and you will remain the biggest so long as you live.

By far the most well-known symptom of Ego is hallucinogenic tendencies. To me best exemplified by the Dunning Kruger Effect. Put simply, the less you know, the more you think you know. It is a lesson in the prevalence of incompetence. Thinking they are the greatest driver alive as they rear-end their neighbor's mailbox. Thinking how easily they could play piano as they struggle to find the chords. Thinking they could walk a tightrope as they trip over their own Ego.

But most of all, most of all! Ego yearns to be heard! It wants to climb to the rooftops and scream into the sunrise! It wants to wake up the city, it wants so badly to be noticed. The feeling of all eyes on it, OH! To Ego there is no feeling greater. It feeds off compliments and lives on attention. If at any time it is not the center of someone else's universe, it will kick and scream and cause a mess until it gets its way. Those of us who have a hold on our Ego can stop the mess. Those whose Ego has a hold on them...Well, they *are* their Ego.

Ego separates people from themselves and each other. That is the tragedy. Ego kills real human connection. It motivates people to see others as tools, and conversations as a means to an end. It separates those with all the power in the world, the financial strength to end world hunger, from those of us who they could save. Ego lets them sleep peacefully in their castle, so disconnected from the rest of us. They end the world as we speak. The reason? They need more. They need to be bigger. Because what their Ego has told them is that it will fill their soul. And that the destruction of our world is an acceptable sacrifice.

Social Media had a hand in the tragedy as well. Young girls find photoshopped models living the dream in Madrid. Anorexia ensues. Young white boys, their egos pushed and shoved from years of bullying and perceived emasculation, succumb to the alt-right pipeline in the scummiest corners of the internet. He's told that his identity gives him power and oppression, the things his ego desires. A strong self-identity, and an 'other' that wants him dead.

Ego pushed them to be 'better'. She is vomiting in the downstairs bathroom. He is sitting in his bedroom, writing his manifesto, as his new online friends tell him how to make a pipe bomb. They have been lost to their Egos. It dribbles down from the crack in her forehead and into the toilet bowl like tears. Those are falling down, too.

BOX
Reegan Craker, 11th grade

Within me lies
comfort
The blue towel that lines my insides is warm and fuzzy
But inside the blue towel
is cold, unmoving
stiff limbs and crumpled fur
The blue towel is lifted from inside of me
rising out
It fell, ever so slightly, revealing eyes
wide open and teeth bared, tongue loose
Quickly the blue towel is wrapped over that face
and they're lowered, both blue towel and limp body
into a ground-box in the brown dirt next to me
The blue is now hiding
turning into brown
as the ground-box is filled
with what I held that morning

RED IN THE WATERCOLOR PALETTE
Alister Easterwood, 12th grade

For a long time I stayed untouched.
My oval shape still in the cheap, white, plastic
bounds that confine me.

I wait for the day stiff bristles will
glide over me, gently dabbing
before smoothing me over a cream white background.

I imagine my hue mixing with lukewarm tap water,
breaking me down in the most
tender way possible.

I see my artist peering down on me,
their gaze full of hesitation and contemplation.
I wish I could soothe them.
Tell them that though I am bold
I am not to be feared.

But all I can do is lie still
and hope that one day they give me
water and a beat-up paintbrush
to tell my story.

A story without words
but instead fiery sunsets on beach waves
and apple trees in open fields.

EXCERPT FROM NOVEL: *DROWNING*
Marisa Marshall, 12th grade

Bellingham.

So much happened in that city.

I remember the exact moment I saw my neighbor's wife talking about how she watched him light himself on fire. It was so graphic. I personally think she was the one to do it.

At the time it happened—his death plastered all over every news station within the state—I was two months away from becoming an adult.

I was sitting in the living room in front of my mother as she ironed my father's clothes. He, like always, was at work and wouldn't be home until later that night when both my mother and I were asleep, and for that I was thankful.

Although her husband committed such a gruesome act before her eyes, the woman—MaryAnn Robinson—stood in front of the cameras unnervingly calm. She did not look as upset as someone would if they were in her position. She witnessed it not even twenty-four hours ago. Her hands were shaking, yes, but something in her eyes was very off-putting.

"He grabbed a bottle of beer off the counter, popping the cap off on the edge of the counter, and poured it down his throat before walking up to the gallon of gasoline near the garage door. I wasn't sure what he was doing as we were in the middle of an argument, and he suddenly seemed so calm. I yelled at him, asking him why he was ignoring what I was saying, but he just kept on with it. Then, he opened the thing and doused himself in gasoline." Her lips were quivering as she spoke, having to take one, two, three seconds, before continuing. "I shrieked as I asked Grant what was wrong with him, but he ignored that too and pulled his lighter out of his pocket...and just like that, he lit himself aflame."

I remember sitting there on the floor, unable to take my eyes from the screen, unable to stop listening to the woman speak, and all I heard were lies. Something deep down inside of me was shouting that she did it.

"I stood there in shock for a moment, not sure what to do, watching his clothes...his skin burn up. He just stood there. Not screaming. Not crying out in pain. His face was emotionless. And by the time I was able to think of a sensible way to handle the situation, it was too late. He was already dead."

A deep frown covered her face; a sob escaped her lips as her shoulders collapsed, her hands wiping at her face, almost as if she was acting. Something about the way she carried herself just didn't feel natural. "We have a five-year-old son. I just can't believe he would do something like that...to me, to our son, to our family."

After that, my mother seemed to have enough of the news, grabbing the remote off the table beside her and shutting off the television.

Ten years later, I sit in Matthew's car, staring at the poster on the window of the gas station. His Audi is parked outside of the building.

There is still that same piece of paper hanging there from seven years ago, the words "A Horrible Tragedy..." plastered over the top of it in bold letters. A picture of Grant Robinson appears just below with words strewn underneath. The paper itself is torn at the corners, stained, and there is a crease down the center of it.

Why is that still there?

What makes it even more strange is that this gas station is not in Bellingham where it happened, but in Connell, a city at least four and a half hours away.

I sigh, rubbing the drowsiness from my eyes with my hands, as I have just woken from a second nap a few moments ago. Matthew isn't in the car with me this time. He must be inside the gas station getting some things or using the bathroom. He didn't bother to wake me up to see if I needed something when he got here. That thought brings a wariness to me.

For some reason, I don't like the thoughts rising in my head, wondering if Matthew is mad at me for how I acted towards him earlier.

Does he have the right to be?

I can't hold it against him if he is. I am not exactly the best at handling affection or comfort. Plus, I would probably be mad at myself too if I was him. He did confide in me, after all, and he most likely wanted me to know that I could do the same with him, but I reacted poorly.

Like he said, maybe he just wants someone close.

I'm not exactly keen on the idea of it, although something deep inside of me wants it just as much.

Shifting in my seat, I peer out the front window of the car, trying to get a glimpse inside the building, but the glass of the doors are covered in a blue tint, making it hard to see through. One of the glass doors opens and out comes Matthew, a phone pressed to his ear.

FORGOTTEN BLADE
Randale McCuien, 11th grade

So why, have I,
been forgotten?
I used to sit
upon a pedestal,
a beautifully
crafted blade,
handed down for generations.
But that all changed when my last master fell in combat.
My once beautifully burnished blade
is now rusted.
My polished cross guard now snapped in two.
My leather grip has now faded away.
Just as my hopes of ever sitting upon my pedestal have.
Perhaps it isn't so bad I guess?
Becoming one with the earth,
returning to where I came from.
But to the heroes who have fallen on this field
even if forgotten the effects of what
they fought for will never disappear.
There is a certain honor
in returning to the soil,
a certain honor in death.
Perhaps it's ok if I,
let go of the resentment.
I'm ok with being forgotten.
I have served my purpose;
this is who I am.
I am free.

ODE TO THE DOVE THAT FLEW AWAY
Lucas McSwain, 11th grade

To someone who echoed to me from afar
    You flew to me with an echo strum to that of a guitar.
    To someone who showed me a new initiative,
    You had a way to soar through the wind, so imaginative,
    portraying a life so free to live.
    Making me wonder what I have to give,
    yet giving me a different life perspective.
To someone who once stood out
    Across the classroom full of chatter,
    I kept to myself, self-focused and quiet,
    And you were curious to see what I thought about,
    Though so fragile and sensitive to anything loud, or even a shout,
    To the exception of your own.
To someone who yourself was so vibrant and abstract
    yet so fearful at the screech of a bat.
    Tossing breadcrumbs to once attract,
    The chilled breeze caressing my hand on a moonlit night,
    I realized it was me who was entrapped.
To someone who through the dimly lit evening seemed so restless,
    Across the geometric pattern houses laid upon the streets,
    Horsing around, running around-
    But you flap your wings,
    Not realizing how careless.
    As time went on, there wasn't a choice but to say less.

Though once the summer weather had assented,
    You migrate and leave south.
    Along so ignorant,
    Seeking warmth to escape your suddenly freezing familiar home.
    The damn within couldn't escape my mouth.
To someone who had to leave,
    Time seems non-existent and amiss.
    This is gratitude and reluctance,
    To grieve through the feeling of a hole, containing a bottomless abyss.

THE REAL NOURISHMENT OF CHILI CON CARNE
Dominic Montoya-Arlt, 11th grade

In a blank white bowl rimmed with blue, there was a mouth-watering pile of sludge-like chili. It was somehow both chunky and watery, like a booger in someone's drink or spoiled cottage cheese. It's a slab of rich, plump beans with veins of white cheese making a meaty corona in its depths. Its smell was something different altogether with that distinct umami scent that promised a strong, filling meal that would still bring me back for seconds. The crackers I ground to meal within it brought the consistency to just that right amount of crunch.

From the narrow kitchen (it was more of a hallway, really) the smell of food would waft out to me at the sandbox and I would shut the water off, put my toy soldiers in a pile and rush inside. My mud-caked arms alerted my mother about the hose being used, but she was never strict with me. She's the kind of soul that finds it hard to raise their voice unless in pure frustration.

When I had chili as a child, my family and I would gather around the television and watch an old DVD that skipped whole chunks of the movie. At that point, we were in my cramped old house and we could wander from the kitchen into the bedroom with half a dozen steps. I don't remember anything about the movies we watched, but I do remember that sometimes we had to use plates instead of bowls because we had so few dishes.

My mother would serve up "bowls" and we'd sit down in the living room on the mishmash of furniture my mother had gotten good deals on. Our kitchen had only three chairs and a round white table barely four feet across, making it suitable only for holding the food. When we were in the midst of moving, chili was nearly all we ate. It was the only thing my mother could make and expect regular enjoyment from my siblings and I. My sisters were a picky bunch and I was a growing child, hitting growth spurt after growth spurt. The meat and beans account for at least a fifth of my height.

The living room that I grew up playing in had this old, crusty black leather armchair that took up a quarter of the room. In the summer, sitting in it meant pasting your back with sweat. Chili was a late winter meal, though, and my sisters and I would wrestle each other out of the armchair to get the prime spot next to the television.

When we were packing up to move, my family survived on chili. Sunday of every week, the house was packed with the hearty smell of chili and the next two days would be leftovers for dinner. It was so cheap, which is probably why it got so popular after it was introduced to the United States. In the 1850s, travelers would pack dried meat and beans and then boil them while on the road, lasting for days on chili. They didn't call it chili, though; to them, it was just another kind of road snack.

The name 'chili' actually comes from the Spanish term 'chili con carne', meaning 'chili with meat' or 'chili with beef' in English, chili being chili peppers. There's a lot of debate over where chili con carne actually originated from, ranging from a nun from Spain who astral-projected and taught it to a Native American tribe to prisons just throwing whatever food they have into a bowl and making a stew out of it.

The story about the nun, Sister Maria de Ágreda, states that this sister had the ability to be at two places at once. While sleeping in her home, she could project her body and appear wherever she'd like. She supposedly converted about fifty Native Americans of the Jumano tribe and also taught them how to make chili. I've eaten plenty of chili and I can verify that you do not get superpowers from that, so something else must have given Sister Maria that power.

Perhaps the more plausible example given is from the account of a Spanish conquistador, Bernal Diaz del Castillo, who states that some of his companions were slain and turned into a stew served with tomatoes and chili peppers. While I'm up for checking the recipe's authenticity, I don't think I'll get the chance any time soon. If you are willing to donate some parts, seek me out personally and I'll put them to good use. I'll even give you priority for sampling the chili.

Well, no matter the origin of chili, it has firmly embedded itself in the minds of Americans as a specifically Mexican dish thanks to the Chili Queens of San Antonio. It should be noted that Mexicans are frankly insulted by the implication that chili con carne comes from their culture. These Chili Queens were primarily middle-to-lower class women of Mexican descent who would serve chili con carne from massive iron pots. Small venues were set up outside of the Queen's houses, with the queen's own chairs and tables set out and her family helping serve the food. People came from all over to taste the chili there and traffic only grew when the religious folk started preaching against it. This tradition started in the 1890s and lasted fifty years, all the way up until new health sanctions were placed and shut down the last of the chili stands.

I can just imagine a raucous group of tourists settling in at a table in front of a chili queen's house, joking and stamping with empty stomachs. A slight, plump Latino woman with her black hair pulled back in a bun sweeps over to the table, balancing four bowls along the nooks and palms of her arms. The bowls are steaming, having just been taken out of the pot, but years of life in the Texas sun has made the woman indifferent to the heat. With a bare bit of restraint, the tourists wait for the chili to cool down before tearing away. The meal is devoured and when the tourists turn to thank the woman with an awkward "gracias" she's already off, stirring the great black pot with a ladle so big that some might consider it a club.

In my mind, there's nothing more beautiful than a person who puts in all of the hard work and receives a thanks they weren't trying to get. I wish I had half of the dedication and a tenth of the satisfaction from when I finished my work. My mother has spent half of her life doing everything she could to keep her children happy and healthy, making all of her decisions with our best interests at heart. As the Chili Queens proved with their history-making friendliness, the real nourishment of chili con carne is the warmth you get, not the meat. That warmth kept me through a rough move and an even rougher winter.

THE DARK RIDE
Mason Moran, 11th grade

The water is oily black. A tar, pitch colored ink wafting against the two pontoons beneath. The boat itself hummed a wispy gurgle, the sharp metal slicing delicately through the lake. I lie on the boat's seat cushions, which had previously been baked by the sun until they one day popped into foamy popcorn.

There are six of us. My aunt and uncle, my sister and nephew, my dad, and me. Many of them reek of booze and thick cigarette smoke. But within lies a prevailing thin scent of fresh lake water. Although mostly intoxicated, we still ride as we have in the light, and as we have done annually for many years. We speak softly as if any louder we would wake the wind, or upset the water, or offend the stars. The bimini hangs over top, and the white fence around the edge of the boat is the only thing keeping any of us from taking a dive. Small lights dot the front of the boat, around where the headlights had been turned on. Although now that the headlights were off, our presence was still obtainable to other vessels and eyes. Around the abyssal lake glowed deck lights of various houses. Like mini lighthouses, making sure we can guess where the land is. I see islands, black blotchy smudges, and we know not to head for them. And when we departed, we made sure not to lose the light that belonged to our house. For if we did, perhaps the boat would have been our place of rest that night. I am blind to all but the sky, with the rest of the world fading into a ghostly version of itself. Barely visible to the shadow filled eye. Stars blanket a bed of darkness, with the moon, an LED lamp so bright, yet so cold, the overseer of the stars. I see the big dipper pouring into the little dipper, as if they are drinking a toast to the night sky. Perhaps the subject of their toast is the northern star at the tip of the little dipper's handle. Although the night is old, the breeze remains warm. We all sleepily gaze up at the kaleidoscope of stars. The light pollution, although very little, appears on the ridge of the sky. So bright you may mistake it for the morning sun rising to greet the unearthly blue sky. And out of the corner of my eye I see it, a dullen fountain of northern lights, clawing at the sky. Faint yet vibrant streaks localized in a stary territory of its very own. The stripes vary and move up and down, slower than any time lapse video on the history channel. So unfortunately faint that only a dank and dull green can shine, like sunlight through a street drainage grate. It feels as if time slows when you stare at it. You start to perceive the slow ebb and flow that accelerates and decelerates at extremely varying tempos. A song written and performed by the sun for the stars. So dull and quietly shone that at one point you may think the lights have stopped in place, just for the next millisecond to show you that the stripes have shot through the sky in an astounding spectacle. Only in the next second will it look as it had. A tiger claws scratch mark on the star filled abyssal sky. As I take it in, I close my eyes.

BEFORE AND AFTER
Abraham Murphy, 12th grade

Before

    Before you fly, you must run
Before you run, you must walk
Before you walk, you must stand

    Before you stand, you must crawl
Before you crawl, you must move
So, you must move to fly

    The only thing you need to do,
Is move an inch to begin your journey.

After

    After you've flown, you fall
After you've fallen, you land
After you've landed, you lie

    Under the ground, you rest
Under the ground, you are missed
Under the ground, you will be remembered

    Forever and on,
Under and after,
You are loved
I will remember you

COFFIN THOUGHTS
Eli Pszczolkowski, 12th grade

They open my padded, hungry stomach,
    maroon like the cloak of a king,
    displaying remains that should be decaying–
    tapestry tales of a life once lived,
    a long life, says the crow's feet clinging to the eyes,
    a sickly life, from the look of the thin and pale skin,
    reduced now to a pointless, unceremonious thing.

Yet still, they don't glance at me more than once,
    my subtle mahogany grain,
    polished to a spotless mirror–
    those black-veiled mourners
    would realize how ridiculous they look
    as they file past,
    tears overflowing and steps comically slow,
    like they don't anticipate the same fate,
    if only they would stop to gaze.

But of course they can't tear their eyes from the corpse,
    that beautified and putrefying
    husk of what once was,
    but unlike the sculptor of my twisting golden floral patterns,
    the mortician's reconstructed the body wrong,
    artificial gums pushing the lips outward, apelike,
    the hair flowing in just the wrong direction,
    a whiff of chemical preservation like lemon and bleach in the nose,
    flaws utterly alien to my measured scentless self.

Now the mourners gather to surround my burial,
    an open maw of earth,
    waiting, drooling beneath me–
    through the storm of icy monsoon,
    the storm of their soggy squelching hugs,
    the storm of whispers of "She lived a good life";
    why do the shadowed figures stay in their little huddled company
    when they perform none of it for me?

I'm lowered into the grave,
    with the chill of choking mud,
    the congregation sobbing, but not at my discarding,
    not my humiliation, not my abandonment,
    will be the last sound I ever hear,
    through the muffled ocean of grainy, slopping clod–
    my mirror surface scratched and stained,
    if I could scream, it'd go unheard.

If the corpse was of any value, I suppose,
I perhaps could pray for a grave robber to dig up both our bones.

A LUMPY BEET
Vincent Redman, 11th grade

The soil was soft
Like a freshly baked cake
Warm in the days, cool in the nights
It was a comforting place to be
No one had to see me
Not the scars on my skin
Or the holes in my body
Scratched by rocks
And eaten by worms

I was ripped from the ground
Heart shaped and bumpy
They cut off my tail
My only limb
They dropped me into a bucket
Filled with icy water
It enveloped me
Bubbles erupted from my tiny mouth
The water changed colors
Red seeping from my tail
It clouded the water
Salt stung my eyes
I couldn't close them
I tried to swim
Instead I sunk
I rolled around the bottom
Trying everything I could to get up
But the walls were too high

And the water too deep
It seeped into every pore
Salt in every cut
Salt in every hole

I want to go home
The hand of a giant reaches for me
It's warm compared to the water below
That knowledge doesn't comfort me
I'm set in a crate
No longer am I thrown around
I see other beets like me
One with a spot for two tails
One with sprouts like a tree
Many with cuts and bruises
Just like me

LOVE IN A DIFFICULT TIME OF BISCUITS: WHY THE LITTLE THINGS MATTER

Madeline Rowney, 11th grade

The sunrise breeze carries a morning dew aroma through an open window; I fall back comfortably onto a padded chair, holstered with a decade-old floral cloth. Cozying into the soft embrace of a barely awake haze, I reach for a ceramic mug on the coffee table next to me. I wince, pulling my hand away from the hot cup, opting to grab it by the handle instead. As I raise the mug to my lips, the steam rises to greet my face. Closing my eyes, I take the first sip of tea.

A peacock, painted bright blues and greens, stares through the glaze at me. I forgot something. I groan, stretching my shoulders back until the blades touch, and stand up. Stalking towards the kitchen, I sulk about my perfect morning being paused. I arrive at the cupboards, reaching up to the second to top shelf, I feel around for my prize. I whisper a shout of victory when my hand finds a crinkly plastic tube. Pulling it down to eye level, I tear at the red strip in the wrapping, creating a circular opening at the top of the tube. I pull out two perfect-grain biscuits. A golden-brown color, with exactly twelve small holes stamped in the cookie and the classic *McVities* logo in the center of each one. I smile absentmindedly, reminiscing on the fond memories of McVities Rich Teas and the loving acts of my mother.

Tea biscuits hadn't always been available to the preschoolers of working-class families. In fact, from their creation in 17th century Yorkshire to around 1850, most people didn't have access to these simple delicacies. Beginning in 1840, a noblewoman named Anna, the seventh Duchess of Bedford, introduced the concept of afternoon tea to the upper-class population of England. The Duchess tended to get hungry around four o'clock, but dinner wasn't served until a fashionable eight o'clock. She began ordering servants to bring her tea, a slice of bread and butter, and occasionally some cake to hold her off until the bigger meal later that evening. The habit became so commonplace that she started inviting friends to join her.

Pretty quickly, the idea of a snack break between lunch and dinner spread across the upper-class people of England. By 1850, nearly every wealthy family hosted daily afternoon tea gatherings. Only wealthy Englishmen were able to take the time to sit down for a snack, as middle-class citizens were far too busy frying off their hands in factories. That was, until the rise of high tea.

High tea was a time for working-class citizens to sit down and decompress from their 14-hour work days, named after the high stools they sat in. Tea biscuits, being primarily wheat and sugar, became a popular treat for those unable to afford the more elaborate desserts. McVities finally united the classes in 1893 when the company received the royal stamp of approval, making the Rich Tea a beloved household biscuit for all levels of society, hence, why a biscuit of noble ancestry ended up in my little hands.

My mom, although still irritated by the biscuit crumbs, really hated when the cookies got wet. The Rich Tea biscuit had the apt nickname of "One-Dips." Hold the biscuit in the cup for more than five seconds, and you will only bring back half the cookie. The other half floated sadly to the bottom of your mug. If you were quick, a spoon and some less-than-adequate fishing skills could get you a very soggy oatmeal-esque mush. However, if you let that lonely other half sit and decay until you finish your drink, a grotesque mixture of pappy cookie pulp and lukewarm tea will be what's left of your last few sips. It's a scheming, guileful concoction. Unassuming at first, you can't even process the violation until it has slithered down your throat and stuck in your teeth and under your tongue. One can imagine the despair I felt seeing my precious biscuit droop into the mug, knowing the only person who could save me was my mom. This being said, I was incredibly, often insufferably stubborn.

"Only dip them once," my mother cautioned, "they'll fall into your mug, and I won't get you a spoon this time."

I always dipped them twice.

As I got older, one might assume I would know the consequences, and I did. But I just kept dipping those nefarious biscuits into my tea. My mom had this quiet understanding of my system. Or maybe she didn't understand at all, but she always got up for me. She always hurried to the kitchen and back, carrying a little pink plastic spoon like it was Excalibur. I'd thank her and promise not to do it again, until the next time, of course. Once, twice-

"Mum, could you get me a spoooooon?"

Christmas Eve, 1914 in a war-torn field on the Western Front, song broke out among German troops. Hymns and carols echoed across the battlefield and into the trenches of the British Army. A solemn rendition of "Stille Nacht" ("Silent Night") took place, and the guns went quiet for the first time since August. The next day, British and German soldiers made their way to No Man's Land, meeting in the middle. They played soccer, exchanged gifts and drinks, and, most importantly: shared spirit. Just a couple of days before, these men were fighting tooth and nail with each other, sworn mortal enemies. But in the misery of trench warfare, they came together to celebrate Christmas. Isn't it beautiful how small acts of kindness can shine like gold in a person's memory? The Christmas Truce of 1914 was only five months into World War I. A few months later, chemical warfare would make its first deadly appearance and would go on to kill and disable an entire generation of men. So much more pain and suffering would happen to those soldiers in Belgium, and many wouldn't survive, but on Christmas Day, 1914, joy could be found in the most miserable places.

Henry Clay once said, "Courtesies of a small and trivial character are the ones which strike deepest in the grateful and appreciating heart." It is not the grand gestures or the big outspoken words of adoration that stick in one's mind. Instead, the small acts of kindness found in day-to-day life end up staying with someone. Whether it be a little pink spoon or Christmas carols sung in the middle of a war, the tiniest bits of love are what give us humanity.

A peacock, painted bright blues and greens, stares through the glaze of my mug at me. My eighth-grade algebra teacher gifted it to me on the last day of school, a note folded and placed neatly inside. I was surprised by the pink and green gift bag he handed me through the car window.

Sparkly white tissue paper was hastily shoved in the bag to cover the gift. To be completely honest, I thought the mug was corny. In gold cursive lettering, the word "stunning" was printed on the inside, and the Target price tag was still stickered to the bottom. I cringed silently, *far from my taste*, I thought. Politely thanking him with a strained smile, my car rolled forward to say goodbye to the next teacher in line.

It wasn't until later that I opened his note. The card couldn't have been more than three inches wide. The cardstock was cautiously bound by smooth red felt. Delicate gold butterflies made indents on the cover, reflecting against the ceramic of the mug. The note itself was short and sweet. He thanked me for attending class all throughout the COVID-19 lockdown. Seeing my face in the little square on his computer engaging while the other students sat with their cameras off, no doubt playing video games or scrolling on their phones, gave him hope that he was still doing his job as a teacher. After I finished reading the note, I cried. Hard. I had no idea how much I had helped him during an insanely difficult time by just being there and wishing him a good day at the end of each class. It was regular human decency, but it meant so much more. The peacock mug is now one of my favorites to drink out of. The painted bird softly watches me as I go about my morning, sitting next to a stack of Rich Tea Biscuits.

THE STORY OF NOTHING, SOMETHING, AND THE BEGINNING
Isabel Schmidt, 11th Grade

Before there was Something, there was Nothing. And when I say nothing, I mean there was Nothing, the god of empty space. Nothing was lonely, so they created Something. Something thought there should be more, there should be more to light up the nothing. Nothing agreed and together, Nothing and Something created Xironia.

Xironia wanted light, so she created the stars. Since there was now light, Nothing and Something let Xironia take care of the nothing and something. After a while of being alone, Xironia decided to create friends. Evo, Dracon, Cygnus, and Leax were created from stars, created as the Brother's. While the new gods loved the stars, they wanted something of their very own.

Xironia created them a planet, someplace they could be the gods of. Evo fell in love with this planet, which was covered in lively greenery. They decided to call this planet Lutum. Dracon, Cygnus, and Leax loved this planet as well, but wanted their own planet.

Xironia created another planet, this one made of lava and fire. Dracon took a liking to this planet almost immediately. He decided to call this planet Ignis.

Cygnus and Leax didn't like either of the planets, and asked for one together. Xironia gave them what she could, a planet of howling wind and cold waters. The waves called to Leax, powerful and cold. The howling wind called to Cygnus, who loved the free and rushing feeling. They decided to call this planet Ventus Aqua.

Xironia loved that her new friends loved their planets, that they could be the gods of something. Leax and Cygnus shared a planet, Evo and Dracon did not. Dracon began to brag about Ignis, about the lava and fire. He spoke about how he could destroy Evo's planet if he so desired.

Leax and Cygnus defended Evo, claiming that if Dracon hurt one planet, he hurt them all. Dracon did not share the sentiment.

Xironia got frustrated with the fighting between the gods, and pushed all the planets together creating Omnis. The planet of All.

"Without one is without all," became Xironia's famous declaration. The Brothers came to the same conclusion, they were one. They were gods.

After they had explored Omnis, and worked together to create a beautiful world, they decided to make little gods. These little gods were not immortal, like the Brother's and Xironia. They could die and get hurt, the gods called them the Mortales.

The Mortales began to worship the Brother's and Xironia, for giving them all they could ever need. Xironia and the Brother's became Saluatores, the saviors.

Saluatores watched over the planet, keeping the Mortales from hurting each other. And to keep the Mortales in control. Saluatores helped the Mortales with agriculture, fresh water, heating, and power.

The Saluatores were the reason the Mortales were created, it would make sense the Saluatores would become the powerful ones. That is the story of Nothing, Something, and the beginning.

FREE FALL
Megan Speers, 12th grade

The blustery wind was
Cold that day,
It curled around my worn,
Flaming edges,
Pulling at my stem,
Which connected to a twisted branch,
And flowed all the way back to her trunk
Of gnarled bark
My branch began to sway,
And her trunk shuddered

Snap

Almost as if to say:
It's time to go

Disconnected

I fell,
Tumbling,
   Rolling,
      Plunging,
Through the biting air

It wasn't the thrilling flight I'd thought of.
It wasn't graceful and light.
I wasn't careening toward the ground,
Toward the rest of the fallen leaves,
But rather toward the hand
Of a little boy.

He reached up and caught me mid-spin,
The warmth of his hands felt comforting
Against my weather-worn edges
As he held me up to the light,
Admiring the colors bouncing on his face.

Past streets filled with rows
Upon rows of white houses,
He skipped home,
Away from the woods,
Away from my home.
(Although I'm not sure if I can call it that anymore)

He ran up the driveway of a big yellow house,
With a yard full of leaf piles,
And golden sun rays.

Up the steps through a slamming door,
Into a warm house,
Filled with homey smells of cinnamon and pumpkin,

Up the steps through a bedroom door,
He opened a leather bound notebook,
And slipped me between the lined pages,
Filled with sketches, haikus,
And other colorful leaves,
Reaching out against the paper,

Almost as if to say:
Welcome home.

THRONE
Alicia Streeter, 11th grade

<u>Cast of Characters</u>

MANNY   A tall man with long, black and white hair. He wears a purple coat with gold trim and fancy clothes. He was once nobility and holds on to that dearly. Very cunning.

ALISTER   Wears raggedy clothes and chainmail armor. He carries a sword and knows how to fight. He's a peasant. He travels around quite often looking for jobs.

KING   He is young. He is kind and giving. He tries to run the kingdom as fairly as possible.

YOUNG MANNY   A young child. He is dirty and poor. He has long black hair. He is timid.

<u>Scene</u>

Lydarusa, a medieval civilization where kings still rule the lands.

<u>Time</u>

In a time similar to the dark ages.

Scene 1

AT RISE: The stage is split in two. Each side mirroring one another. One representing the past and the other the future.

On the right side is ALISTER. He is slumped against an old church building.

On the left is YOUNG MANNY who is leaning against the same church but a past version.

The light over the right half of the stage is dim. Trumpets blare from off stage

KING walks onto the left side of the stage.

YOUNG MANNY frantically tries to pull his hair up in the presence of the king.

The KING stops and looks at YOUNG MANNY.

KING
What are you doing?

(YOUNG MANNY freezes)

KING
I'm not going to cut off your head for being unkept.

                    YOUNG MANNY
                    O-oh.

          (KING chuckles and takes the hair piece out of his
          hair and hands it to YOUNG MANNY)

                    KING

Come to pray with me?

                    (beat)

Seems like you might need it right now...

                    (beat)

Because- oh, never mind. What are you doing out here alone anyways? You look young to be lonely.

                    YOUNG MANNY
                    Why... um- just sitting.

                    KING
                    What about your family?

(beat)

Oh... I see.

          (Lights fade on the left and brighten on the right.
          MANNY enters and notices ALISTER)

                    MANNY
                    What happened to you?

>   (beat)
>
>   Don't be such a... here.
>
>   (MANNY throws a flask of water at ALISTER'S feet)
>
>   ALISTER
>   I don't want your fancy liquor.
>
>   MANNY
>   It's not. Just water.
>
>   (ALISTER hesitantly takes a drink from the flask)
>
>   ALISTER
>   ...Thank you
>
>   MANNY
> So? What happened to you?
>
>   ALISTER
> I'm looking for work.
>
>   MANNY
> Oh, really? You-
>
>   ALISTER
> Don't.
>
> MANNY
>   I wouldn't call you such things.

ALISTER

Mhm.

MANNY

So, you live in Lydarusa?

ALISTER

What? Why? Recruiting troops or something? What business do you have here with those fancy clothes?

MANNY

Calm down. I'm not going to take you anywhere you don't want to go.

(Beat)

You're a good man, right?

ALISTER

Don't patronize me ric-

MANNY

I didn't call you nasty names. I request the same courtesy.

(pause)

ALISTER

I wasn't.

MANNY

Mhm.

(All lights brighten.)

KING and MANNY
(Speak in unison.)

I might be able to help you...

(Lights fade on right.)

KING

Why don't you come pray with me?

(beat)

Come on! I've always wanted to know the perspective of someone like you.

YOUNG MANNY

Why?

(pause)

KING

Well, my older brother... It's a long story. I'll tell you after we pray.

(KING holds his hand out for YOUNG MANNY. Lights fade back to MANNY and ALISTER. ALISTER sits up more.)

ALISTER

What?

MANNY

Yes, yes. You'll do perfectly. So, you know how to use that sword of yours?

ALISTER
Of course. What good is a peasant who can't defend his kingdom?

MANNY
Wonderful, wonderful...

(MANNY holds his hand out to ALISTER. ALISTER takes it and pulls himself up.)

(BLACKOUT)

Scene 2

AT RISE: ALISTER and MANNY enter.

ALISTER is holding a flask and a newspaper.

There's a small fireplace and belongings around. The only light source is a dim blue light from the moon and the light from the fireplace.

ALISTER
Why did you ask me to do this, exactly?

MANNY
Hm... what's in that flask?

(ALISITER hands the flask over.)

ALISTER
Was it really over a small inconvenience? You guys sounded close.

(MANNY takes a sip from the flask and spits it out.)

MANNY
This is just water!

(He throws the flask at ALISTER'S feet.)

ALISTER
Why did you hire me exactly?

(beat)

I don't have to do this you know.

MANNY
Yes, you do. There's nothing else you can do. I think I understand more about you than you think. We aren't-

ALISTER
Don't compare me to you.

MANNY
Don't pretend like we're all that different. It doesn't matter why. The king was like a brother to me and he put a bounty on my head. He deserves what's coming to him. You'd do it even if he didn't.

(ALISTER remains silent and MANNY rises.)

ALISTER
Don't pretend like you understand.

MANNY
I'm going to get something from the pub.

(MANNY walks out.)

ALISTER

For god's sake.

(ALISTER sits.)

I knew this didn't feel right. He's a liar. It says it right here.

(ALISTER pulls out the newspaper.)

How could he call the king a brother and still do what he did? I know this isn't right but... what else can I do? He doesn't understand my situation... He can't understand. I'm not like him...

(pause)

I've never killed before. I don't know if I can even go through with this. What other options do I have though? I've traveled so far and still... nothing. I need food and... what if he does deserve it?

(pause)

What if Manny is right? What if I am like him?

(pause)

Does it even matter?

(ALISTER picks up the flask and peers at his reflection in it.)

God, help me...

(BLACKOUT)

Scene 3

AT RISE: It's late in the evening. A few days have passed and it's after the assassination of the king.

MANNY stands in a castle holding a bloody crown.

In front of him are steps leading to the throne room. There is a large spotlight on the throne.

MANNY

It's right there.

(ALISTER enters and looks around, amazed at the beauty of the palace. His clothes are bloodied.)

ALISTER

After all this time...

MANNY

Yes... after all this time.

(MANNY steps over to ALISTER and hands him the bloodied crown.)

MANNY

It's all yours. Everyone's going to love you.

(ALISTER takes the crown.)

I'm surprised. I thought you couldn't do it. You remind me a lot of myself...

(MANNY steps onto the first step, hungrily reaching for the throne.)

ALISTER

This isn't right.

(The spotlight on the throne flickers out)

MANNY

What?

(MANNY stops and turns to ALISTER. He steps off the first step.)

MANNY

This is it. We finally made it.

ALISTER

I should go home.

MANNY

We- you are finally home

ALISTER

No.

MANNY

We have to do this.

ALISTER

No.

MANNY

We worked so hard.

(pause)

ALISTER

I want to go home.

MANNY

Don't say that. I did everything to get you here.

ALISTER

No...

(in a whisper.)

I can't believe I let you talk me into this.

MANNY

What? You agreed to this.

ALISTER

You lied to me! You killed his son!

(ALISTER throws the newspaper on the ground.)

MANNY

Shut up! I did what I had to! You're not so innocent!

(MANNY picks up the newspaper and scans over it.)

You knew for this long and you still went through with it?

                        ALISTER

I didn't want to believe it...

                        (beat)

I needed... this isn't my fault! I didn't have a choice.

                    (MANNY steps over to ALISTER. ALSITER grabs the handle to his sword and drops the crown. ALISTER moves to stab MANNY. He stops himself.)

                        MANNY

You're just as bad as I am.

                        ALISTER
                    (He lowers his sword.)

I thought...

                        MANNY

You thought what? That you could somehow win? You should know by now you can't.

                    (MANNY gestures to ALISTER'S raggedy clothes.)

                        MANNY

Peasant.

ALISTER

Shut up! You have no idea what it's like! I pray every night. Every single night. This was supposed to be my break!

MANNY

Then you are a fool!

ALISTER

No!

MANNY

Yes! I grew up just like you. Every night I sat by my bed praying God would someday answer me. But no. I weaseled my way into my fine wealth. I didn't need God's hand. I played their little game and look! I still lost. I ran this kingdom better than anyone ever could. I was great. And look! I still lost! And now I'm here, pleading with the likes of you, someone who never had the judgment to get themselves somewhere great. I know somewhere deep inside of you you're just as bitter as I am. You killed my kingly brother and yet you still believe you're better than me. Why? Because of your sorrow? As if I have never wept with regret. As if emotion was akin to your action. Does your poor status relieve you from repercussions? As if I hadn't grown up just like you? So now that I'm rich, I am no longer human? Now that I have played into their hands, now that I have relinquished my humanity to status quo, I am no longer a peasant? As if I'm not the same young boy who wept by his bed praying his life away. As if God ever answered me!

(pause)

So, regret would've made me better?

(pause)

But you know what? I do not regret what I have done. Because maybe I did it for myself, but so have you. We are one in the same. And even so, our history books will regard you as the hero. Because I chose this path for you. I deceived you into killing my brother, right? So, tell me, dear *brother* of mine, what makes you a hero? Is it your regret? Does that make you someone to look up to? Is it your path to greatness? As if I hadn't paved it? Is it your innocence, your vigor, your passion? Because you're the underdog? Or maybe, is it because history needs a hero? Is that not giving into status quo?

(MANNY steps closer and ALISTER drops his sword. MANNY kicks the sword away.)

You are not the hero the peasants will see you as.

(MANNY grabs the crown and leaves. Once MANNY is out of sight ALISTER follows after. He stops just before he exits and turns back to the sword. He walks back and picks it up.)

ALISTER

I'll do what I have to... Just like you.

(Lights flicker red. He follows MANNY off stage.)

(BLACKOUT)

ALL ALONE
Yahir Torres, 12th grade

In control but never making change. Killing

The world to make money from the willing

Who don't understand that the rich don't care.

The everyday person wouldn't dare

To speak out about the days without rest.

The days without food or water. Some protest

To try and make a change but still end

With Starbucks in hand, using Amazon to spend

What little they have left. The ones in control

Will never know how much they have really stole.

The powerful need to know what life is like

For the people that give them theirs. The spiked

Fences that separate these lives,

Paid for by the ones on the other side.

The powerful, the rich, the people that are never shown

Are the ones that own the world, all alone.

TIME AT THE CORE
Gabrielle Vermilya, 11th grade

The apple juice was always warm. The very smell of it reminds me of my brother and me, when we were still young, and innocent, and wet the bed while we dreamed of dinosaurs and Indiana Jones. We'd spill the juice on our baby blankets, and the smell of the juice would lure us to sleep with our blankets snuggled up against our tiny, sleepy bodies. That was before we were too old for those blankets. That was before we moved clockwise.

The apple juice was never in a glass. It was always in a colorful, cheap plastic cup with a lid that never matched. Who could afford real glasses when you had five children and a dog? Especially when the first four kids were clumsy girls and the youngest was a boy who loved to mess with his big sisters. When Mom bought new big-kid cups at the mall everybody used those ones instead, but I always had to have the old red one with the blue lid, or the blue one with the green lid, or the yellow one with the purple lid. I used those until I was ten. I didn't want to move clockwise and use glasses like other kids.

The apple juice always stood on the table under the TV, right next to where I slept on the floor in Mom and Dad's room. I used to sleep in there because I was scared, but then it just became my routine. My brother's routine, too. His cup rested on my mom's side table. Late at night, his tiny hands, two years younger than mine, reached from the floor to grab his warm apple juice, in that cheap plastic cup. That was before we started sleeping in our own rooms. Stopped drinking apple juice.

The apple juice always seems to run out late at night, when I woke up with dreams of waterfalls and running rivers, and I had to wake Mom up to ask her to fill it. She's never happy late at night. But my young self only knew that when she finally came back, the apple juice was cold and fresh. That was before I moved clockwise and drank water when I woke up thirsty in the night. Before I got it myself.

The apple juice brings up memories of the TV. Of late night medical shows every Tuesday and Thursday, and comedies I wouldn't understand for years every Saturday. The times when I should've been asleep, dreaming of SpongeBob instead of watching Mom's shows. When we woke up in the morning, Mom filled our cups with fresh juice. Then, us kids would sit in front of the TV in our dad's old shirts and Pullups while the dog crunched her kibble in the next room and cartoons taught us lessons we'd remember for life. That was before we moved clockwise and everyone was watching their phones instead of the TV. That was before we learned to hold our pee when we slept, like the big kids.

The apple juice was fresh and new on Sunday mornings, when Dad woke up earlier than everyone else. He'd always fill our cups before he left with his button up shirt, glasses he always had to adjust, and the big old fancy Bible, ready to teach. At least Dad never moved clockwise. He always kissed Mom before he left. Before I moved clockwise, I'd kick off my blanket when he wasn't looking so he'd always put my blanket back over me and kiss my head before he left. We'd see him in about two hours anyway, standing on the stage, in the late service. Nobody could get five children to wake up early for church. Not even Mom's force. She moved clockwise, too.

The apple juice was always in the fridge at Grandma's. The fridge that our tiny hands could barely reach. Grandma always bought a brand new bottle of juice and a new jar of Nutella when we came to visit. I'd wake my brother up after our parents fell asleep and we'd sneak downstairs and eat a spoonful of the chocolaty spread and sip apple juice while the clock moved forward past our bedtime. My brother would smile with his chocolaty teeth at our trouble making. That was before he grew taller than me. Before he became too cool to be with his big sister.

The apple juice was enjoyed by everyone. All five kids, even the dog, who would lick the tile floor clean of the spills we made, or lick our sticky apple flavored hands while we slept so we could let her out to pee. The house was always quiet while the dog was out peeing and I was staring out the sliding glass door in princess pajamas and holding a sippy cup of apple juice, watching the old dog run around. That was before Gypsy moved clockwise. That was before her clock broke, and the hands stopped moving. Before so many other clocks broke.

I used to drink apple juice, back when I was a kid. Back before my taste buds changed and it grew sour. Before new clocks were made and started ticking. Long before our new puppy's clock or a new baby's clock started ticking, and started moving forward far too quickly. Back before I was sentimental, or I had anything to be sentimental about. Back before photos meant anything, and I'd scribble all over them with pens. Back before time meant anything, when there was no past or future, only that moment when the apple juice was warm, or gone, or filled back up again. Back before apple juice meant anything to me, like it does now.

THE LIFE OF A GLASS CONTAINER
Aubrey West, 11th grade

I am what you might call a glass container.
I am still most of the time.
I carry 30 gallons of water every day.
Within this water, there are 14 fish that I personally
Take care of.
I am the primary source keeping these little creatures
Alive.
It is my responsibility and I firmly believe
That
If anything happens to the fish I am to blame,
Unfortunately.
I never rest.
The keeper of these fish is always exhausted,
Always carrying 30 gallons of water,
Carrying the worry whenever a new person walks into the room.
If I'm dirty I can't do anything about it,
Algae sticks to the walls and creates a horrifying smell.
My water will turn almost a milky color,
Bad enough that sometimes you won't be able to see the fish.
It can get very embarrassing sometimes.
I don't get a break.
I am still, I cannot walk or run.
I never have privacy when people decide to come in
And look at me with no permission.
I am constantly taking care of things.

It's tiring.

But it doesn't mean I don't enjoy what I do.

I have cared for these little creatures for quite some time now,

And I have grown a love for them; my love for each no more profound than for another.

I care for them, and I stick by them.

It is my responsibility to take care of them;

If anything happens to them, I am to blame.

Photo by Jonas Carlson

Building Stories
2023 Class

INSTRUCTOR INTRODUCTION: BUILDING STORIES

Karin Killian

Writing is a private art. We sit alone, and construct worlds with words. In many ways, this privacy allows us freedom to play and experiment. However, without readers our labor can feel invisible and isolating.

Peer readership is also critical to the process of learning to write fiction. In order to successfully revise our own work, we need trusted readers to reflect back to us what we have accomplished and to help us uncover the untapped potential of our first drafts. We writers call this "workshopping." This is not an easy task. To workshop successfully, writers need to be conscious of setting aside their own egos and approaching their friend's work from a place of radical generosity.

In our last two weeks of class the students in Building Stories learned how to workshop, and then practiced what they learned. I teach the workshop process through a system I call "The three P's." The P's stand for: *Properties, Potentials and Possibilities*.

Properties are what actually made it onto the page, what the reader reads and understands. It's funny how often this drastically contrasts with what the writer intended. Thus, properties feedback, simply hearing how others read and understand the words we assembled, can sometimes be the most helpful for a writer. Especially when we realize there were elements to the story in our mind that we did not successfully illustrate—YET! *Potentials* are latent qualities, tiny bits that came out in the first draft that could contain incredible power if developed further. Every first draft has them, these weird little character details, switches in tense, or leaps in point of view, that were completely accidental, but function as essential portals to the most important elements of the story when further explored in revision. *Possibilities* are ways your reader might imagine the story being developed or expanded in a future draft. This is not prescriptive dictation of an assignment, but generous and caring collaborative brainstorming that allows the artist to witness other people's excitement for their work, which they can take with them as they return to their desks to write the next draft.

Before workshopping each other's stories, the students practiced the "Three P's" method by workshopping a published short story of mine that I know has many flaws. Their feedback was fantastic. And they did an incredible job of supporting each other with ideas and inspiration for subsequent drafts.

I am so impressed with the wisdom and imagination of these students, and absolutely cannot wait to read what they write next!

THE PAINTER'S PORTRAIT
Liam Faunce, 9th grade

I'm standing in a silent art gallery, staring at a painting that reminds me of someone I once knew. I've brung my old, shattered ipod-that thing still works even in 2023!—listening to the entire Rumors album by Fleetwood Mac for the fourth time this week. As I'm staring at the similar green eyes of the woman in the painting, as I'm preparing for the chorus in a song, it's all too much to take in. Emotions, all at once.

Phoebe Everest. I met her back in the seventh grade. She was blonde. She had hazy green eyes and a fair complexion that some may have looked at her and immediately assumed she was just a normal girl. That was the typical standard of beauty, anyways. You're "pretty" so you must be healthy and happy; you're "ugly" so you're unhealthy and unhappy. But Phoebe was my friend. I knew her true beauty. And once you had gotten to know her, *really* know her, her face soon just became more of a blur, and the only thing you could pay attention to was her soul. Her interests, her aspirations. She was the most entertaining girl I've ever known. Her hair was usually put up in difficult braids that she learned to do from books. The haze of her green eyes soon transferred to emerald treasures. Her very personality made her physicality shapeshift into the greatness that reflected upon it. She was truly abstract, a painter's portrait.

As I take in the memories amongst the somehow nostalgic painting and music, suddenly it's 2003 in our sophomore year, Elk Rapids. Now I'm back in *her* room. The creamy walls; the jewelry strewn on tablecloths; the old fashioned candles being the only supporting light; and a big mirror reflecting her bed; the stereo scratching through all the vintage albums from Smashing Pumpkins to Led Zeppelin and to, of course, our favorite album of all: Rumors by Fleetwood Mac. She would imitate Stevie Nicks even though she looked not in the least similar to her, while I'd be the bassist, and we would jump and jump on her big bed while singing, until the very end of a song we'd collapse back into fluffy blankets and sheets.

Whenever I spent the night at her house I would lose track of time. Literally I would close my eyelids and open them five minutes later to a pool of sunlight. No sleep deprivation existed in her territory. I loved waking up in her bed, a reminder I wasn't home. Home was the nightmare that I couldn't sleep through. Phoebe was the comforting reminder saying "it's just a dream."

I loved everything about her house, how it stood three stories tall with big, double-hung windows and how whenever I stepped inside, I could smell food cooking from the kitchen and the scented swirls of poultry or potatoes climbing up every inch of the stairs and the rooms. Yes, Phoebe was rich. And maybe the other people used that as an excuse for being "just like the others." But I know she couldn't concentrate back in grade school and would have to count to 1, 2, 3 a bunch of times just to breathe. She said the world took up too much space. That money couldn't save you from dissatisfaction with everything. And albeit anxious, she would cure the feelings with reading and movies and baking. She was so cultured. Her family took her on trips every year across the world so that she learned different languages and foods. Things like that separated her from the girls at school. But overall, she felt decent about everything.

Until *that* party happened. The party that changed people like her. It was at a neighbors house, supposed to be a college party only but you knew the host for years. Or forever, actually. Nicky Sparker, his name was. Four years your senior, like an older brother. Grew up in the neighborhood together. And also your parents had trust in the community, so we were absolutely welcomed.

The party was big and hot and steamy and there were older people talking to us as if we were their age. The girls complimented our dresses and makeup, and suddenly midway through a conversation with an early twenties blonde, Nicky pulled Phoebe away.

"Hey, can I talk to you?" he said. I didn't remember much after that. I suppose the warning signs were quite obvious. And I should've known. I should have kept track of time of how long she was in the room for, or followed her. After that weekend o, the next week was when the letdown began, I think. That's when you weren't answering the phone much or was "using the bathroom" when really, I knew, you were cutting. Before you told me what had happened at the party and what made you so solemn-the answer being something that would open another portal in our relationship I never knew ever existed, but would need to have time to prepare for-you confessed about your self-harming. You told me during our freshman year after taking a week off school. You were frightened to tell me, but you said it was rather a compulsion to other fears. And I never knew what her fears were. Now it's summer before junior year. We live off chips and barbecues and family-only- parties and late night swims in the creek. You put on such a good show. Your smile, so real. How could I have known you were only getting worse? Anyhow, me and you seemed confident with our lives. We applied to several colleges, waiting for our acceptances. But the last day I ever saw you was when Nicky Sparker came to hang out with us. We were swimming at the creek, but you kept your face half hidden upon water as you observed me and Nicky talking to each other. You just nodded and mumbled whenever he tried speaking to you. Then we play hide and seek around the lake. *Ready or not, here I come.* Then one, two, three, four, sundown. We still can't find you. Until a woman is screaming and your body is glowing pale amongst the moonlight and inky water. You're an alien.

I didn't get answers until later on at the funeral. I went to your bedroom, alone. Scavenging every foot of the room, until I find a crinkled blue and red lined paper in your drawer, reading *Nicky Sparker raped me.* Everything was a blur then. I don't even remember reporting the incident as much as just being paralyzed. You know, I still picture you sometimes when at the beach. Reincarnated to a mermaid and then you, using some magical powers to bring me gills so I too could live in the waters with you too. Forever. So I too could end this one miserable journey called life with her.

I take out my earbuds and try to let my eyes away from the woman in the painting. But somehow I can't. The painting is more specifically a mermaid with long, blonde hair and green eyes. That's why it reminds me of Phoebe so much. Because this artwork, whomever person created it, has linked to my consciousness so unintentionally, so coincidentally, that I aspire to be just like them. I will write a book, or paint a picture. I need to let Phoebe's story out. *Our* story out. Because every artifact, every picture, almost everything shows something we thought we could always keep hidden.

BURNING ICE
Kristen May, 11th grade

My heart pounds, the beat filling my ears, crowding my head. *Thump. Thump. Thump.* My leg bounces and my fingers twitch, itching to punch my leg, punch the pain away, but I can't, not without getting looks, not without the instructor asking me if I'm okay, my parents wondering what's wrong with me, if I belong somewhere else. It felt like the heat was rising in the room, going up and down as if it was music, as if it was a crescendo, the notes dancing around my head, slowly, intently, driving me insane. I itch to knock them away, beat them until they're crumpled and weak, struggling to raise their bodies, crippled notes. Can't do that either though. Can't do that without being questioned. Already on thin ice. Ice ice, falling through. I wonder how long it would be until I passed from hypothermia, the cold sinking into my bones, sinking in until it becomes hot, hot, too hot. Falling. A raging fire, roasting me from the inside out, until I'm nothing but a pile of bones, a pile of bones to be brushed aside. Tossed aside, as I've been my entire life. My leg bounced harder and harder, until I bounced too high and I knocked into the table, a sharp *crack* echoing around the room. I froze and dared a look around, expecting dozens of eyes on me. No eyes. Not one eye. Nobody noticed, too preoccupied with each other and themselves to bother with me, to care, even for one moment, one small, insignificant moment, how I'm doing. Selfish. So worried about themselves, no one realizes that everyone around them is drowning, sinking down down down. Too obsessed to realize that they're sinking too. Everybody's sinking. Sinking into ice. Cold ice. Hot ice. Burning, burning. My eyes blur and I try to focus. Can't. Too late. Too empty. Nothing to keep me tethered any longer. I fall, spinning through the universe, stars rushing, and in each of these stars I see a family, a couple, a person with their dog, a book, a friend. Everyone happy. Content. I reach out, straining, straining, desperately reaching, but I miss every time. Never meant to be happy, I am. Never never never never. Sinking, sinking, sinking. I continue to spin, time dashing by, but I don't care. Not anymore. Too late. Too much ice. Wrapping its slithery hands around me, frigid fingers sinking into my arms, digging holes through my skin. Too cold. Burning ice.

Photo by Jonas Carlson

NWS Scholarship Winners and Honorable Mentions

In partnership with the Grand Traverse Regional Community Foundation

INTRODUCTION FROM GINA THORNBURY
Grand Traverse Regional Community Foundation

The National Writers Series Scholarship competition is made possible through a partnership with the Grand Traverse Regional Community Foundation and the generosity of several local donor partners. The partnership began in 2010 and the contest is held annually for high school students in our five-county region. Students are invited to submit in one of the four contest categories; poetry, fiction, non-fiction and journalism. To ensure an equitable process, a team of judges specializing in each of the genres completes a blind review, and selects a winner and runner-up in each category. Four $1,000 scholarships are awarded to the winners in each genre annually.

WHAT IS YOUR PURPOSE?
Navaeh Wharton, 12th grade
Honorable Mention in Fiction

"What is the meaning of life to you? What is your purpose in life?" I stare at the big bold words that lay across my screen. I have reread the same two questions a hundred times, and each time they burn my cornea, pushing themselves past my iris and branding themselves in my pupil. It hurts to read the question; it hurts even more to process it.

What is my purpose? What is the meaning of life?... How am supposed to know?

I'm only a seventeen-year-old girl who is just trying to plan for college. I sigh and slide my cursor over to another tab. **"Why you? What makes you deserve this scholarship?"** I roll my eyes at the words. *I don't know... I barely even know why I had toast this morning.* I close the tab only to come face to face with another question. **"Tell us something about yourself no one else knows?" "Where do you see yourself in 5 years?" "How do you define failure?" "Who are you?" "What awards have you won?" "What do you consider the most urgent problem in the world today and why?"**

Question after question they burn into my mind, weighing me down. I close my computer and warily glance toward the pile of homework I still haven't done. I groan and stand up, stalking over to my closet. I slip out of my work clothes and into sweatpants and a t-shirt. I grab my pile of homework and plop down at my desk again. Sleep weighs my eyelids and I glance at the clock, 10:00 pm. *I have to finish this before midnight in order to get a solid amount of sleep.* I put my headphones in, the music chasing my thoughts away, allowing me a chance to tackle my homework.

Before I know it, the clock reads 2:00 am. I groan, sliding my headphones off, and quickly finish the last of my homework, scribbling down anything my brain can conjure. I stand up, stretch my limbs, and drag myself to bed. I set my alarm clock before allowing my eyelids to droop and letting sleep devour me. It feels as if I have been dreaming for five minutes when the blaring sounds of my alarm scream at me to get up. I groggily rise and get dressed for school.

In the kitchen, my mom sits at the counter with a cup of coffee. Her black robe is tied tight, and her disheveled hair is pushed out of her face. She smiles at me with sleepy eyes.

"Morning sweetheart." She nods to an empty cup in front of her. "You want some coffee?"

"Yes please." I pour myself a cup and stir in some creamer.

"Want to see a movie tonight? Me, you, dad, and Ethan?"

"Can't. I'm working." I cringe, bringing the steaming cup to my lips. I blow on it slowly, before risking a sip. The hot liquid burns my tongue, the pain flowing all the way down my throat, and I slowly set my cup down.

"Again? Haven't you been working a lot this week?"

"Not really." I shrug, letting my lie slip easily through my lips. "Besides, I need the money."

"For school?"

"Yes." I sigh and bite the inside of my cheek. "Anything in the mail yet?"

"You know you'll probably get an email before you receive anything in the mail."

"Probably." I glance at the clock and dump my coffee out. "I have to get going, have fun at the movie." I plaster a smile and make my way out of the kitchen.

"Don't worry about money please, sweetheart." She calls at me and I say nothing in return. *Says the one who won't help me with college tuition. I am the one who has to pay for every last penny of my education.* I roll my eyes, slide on my shoes, and bound out of my house to my car.

The silence on the way to school allows my thoughts to drift freely, taunting me.

Why me? What is my purpose in life? What is the meaning of life? Do I even have a purpose? I sigh and turn up my music in an attempt to silence the heavy questions.

Should I know the answers to those questions? Am I supposed to know? I pull into the school and rest my head against the steering wheel. *Why me? What is my purpose in life?*

A slam on my window makes me jump up, chasing my thoughts away. I look in alarm to see Liam and Rylee grinning from the other side of my window. I let out a breath before rolling it down.

"Gotcha!" Liam laughs and I roll my eyes.

"Very funny."

"Come on, we're heading inside." Rylee nods to the school and I roll my window up before grabbing my bag and locking my car. Together the three of us walk inside, Liam on my right and Rylee on my left.

"Did you finish the AP Lit and Comp homework?" Rylee asks.

"Only took me about two hours." I turn to her. "Did you?"

"I only got half of it done, I didn't understand any of it." I glance at Liam.

"What about you? Did you finish it?"

"Didn't even start." He grins and shrugs it off. "I'll be fine though; I have a good idea of what the test is on."

"Says the one who got a D last time." I laugh and he gives me a light shove as we shuffle through the doors, dodging the pushy kids. "Want to go to the park for lunch today?" I peer over a few heads, tossing the question to them.

"Yes!" They both answer in unison, and I smile, waving my goodbyes before heading to class. The day goes by fast, with teachers lecturing and students daydreaming; lunch arrives in no time. I meet Liam and Rylee at my car, unlocking it.

"Just push my work clothes aside," I toss to Liam while hopping in the driver's seat.

"You're working again?" "Yeah, why?"

"You've worked every day this week. It's Friday night Eva, take a break." Rylee nods in agreement and I shrug off their concern.

"I need the money for school," I grumble saying nothing more and driving to the park just down the street.

We sprawl our lunches out on the picnic table, soaking in the sun and warm weather. A cool breeze brushes past me and the sound of laughter from the play structure fills the air. I turn at the sound and watch as a parent chases a giggling toddler around the slide. I smile at her laughter, at her innocence and free mind. *I was like that once. What was the meaning of life then? What was my purpose then?* I turn back to Liam and Rylee, sharing a cup of ranch with their carrots and peppers. *What is my purpose now?*

Am I supposed to have a concrete answer to that question? Does anybody? I let out a small sigh and raise my chin to the blazing sun. Its heat washes over me, flushing my cheeks. I bask in the sunlight, allowing its warmth to pebble my forehead with sweat.

"Want to go jump in the lake?" I ask without thinking. I lower my head and glance at my two friends. My cheeks are warm, and my hands are sweaty. They both raise an eyebrow at me and frown. I gaze at the glittering water that lies a few feet away from us.

"Right now?" Rylee questions and I shrug.

"Why not?"

"We still have classes to go to." She checks the time on her phone.

"And?" I shrug. "I'm hot." I rise and grin at the two. "Race ya!" I break into a sprint and listen as their laughter chases me through the scorching sand and into the frigid water. A gasp erupts from my lungs as the water sends an icy chill down my spine. It seeps through my clothes, soaking every inch of my body.

Laughter fills my ears and I turn to see Liam and Rylee drenched and splashing each other. A smile breaks my face and I sink to the bottom of the lake. I push past the crisp water and sit cross-legged on the bumpy ridges in the sand. My hair floats around me, like octopus tentacles reaching out. I open my eyes reaching out to the blurry water, I play with my hair, twirling and twisting strands around my finger. The silence soothes me, dissipating all my stress and exhaustion. I sit there, the piercing water chilling my body and leaving goosebumps across my skin. I let the silence devour me, allowing my mind to rest.

I stay there until my lungs begin clawing at my throat, begging to breathe. I break the surface gasping for air. My friends both float on their backs and smile when they see me. My numb body absorbs the warmth from the sun and my rapid heartbeat echoes in my ears. I take a deep breath and smile. I feel new and alive; I feel free and bold.

I lay on my back and join my two friends. I close my eyes and let the sun wash over my freckles. When we cannot wiggle our toes any longer and our teeth are chattering, we drag ourselves out. The three of us soaking, trudge back to the picnic table. Wet sand clings to our bodies, itching and uncomfortable. We collapse at the table before breaking into a giggling fit.

"That was crazy, I don't know why I did that with you." Rylee laughs and Liam nods agreeing.

"It was spontaneous." I grin. "And adventurous."

"No, you know what will be adventurous?" Liam says nodding to my car. "Sitting in class soaking wet."

"Nooo." Rylee rests her head on the table. "That is going to be so uncomfortable."

"But we can do it." I smile, picking up our trash and grabbing my keys. "Come on, let's go." They shuffle into my car, careful not to soak my seats. I roll down my windows and they both stick their heads out for the ride back to school. The rest of the day goes by fast, regardless of the many odd looks we receive from classmates.

After school I find myself calling out from work and heading home. I run into Ethan, Dad, and Mom when I open the door, they are all dressed and ready for their movie.

"Eva!" Ethan smiles rushing forward to give me a hug. I wrap my arms around his tiny body, giving him a squeeze before he wiggles free.

"You're home early. What about work?" Mom asks.

"Called off, I decided I need a break." She smiles, nodding in agreement.

"Well, do you wanna join us?" Dad holds up a spare ticket.

"I'd love to." I grin and tell them to wait up while I run upstairs to change out of my damp clothes. Before rushing out of my room, I hesitantly open my computer. The question flashes back at me. **What is the**

meaning of life? What is your purpose?" The bold words stare back at me. I wait for the dread and the weight of the question to fill me, but it doesn't. I smile before turning and bounding down the stairs to join my family.

This is my purpose. It's to live, to cry, to laugh, to stress, and relax. The meaning of life is to live it. To question it, to try new things, and to be spontaneous. The purpose of one's life is whatever one chooses it to be. I am the one in control; I am the one that makes decisions for myself, I am the one who chooses whether to overwork myself or not. I am the one who chooses to let things hold me back or not. Right now, I choose to live; I am, after all, the living one.

THE MOON AND BACK
Lucy Ettawageshik, 12th grade
First Place in Fiction

"Milk, eggs. Oh-" There's slight static as Colette fumbles with the phone. "Sorry.

Dropped the list. Cinnamon."

"And pickles," he adds regretfully.

"Yes, and pickles," she says in a relieved tone.

"Gross," he says. She scoffs, and he hears static again as she switches the phone from one ear to the other. He pulls into the parking lot.

"Anything else? I'm heading in."

"Nope. Love you. To the moon-"

"-And back," he finishes. He hangs up. The grocery store is quiet, since it's a Tuesday morning. The sky's a deep gray, clouds heavy with rain. He feels the drops sprinkle his shoulders as he walks back to the car, peppering his gray blazer with darker gray circles. He drives home in near silence, Colette's favorite jazz station playing softly in the background.

His phone dings.

He glances down briefly, thinking it's Colette. It's not. He frowns at the unknown number and picks up the phone, half glancing at it, giving most of his attention to the impatient red car behind him that doesn't seem to like turn signals very much.

NEW ASSIGNMENT, the text reads.

He pulls over.

Who is this? He responds.

They type back immediately.

You know who it is.

He slams his hand not holding his phone down on the steering wheel, the sharp spike of pain momentarily distracting him from his cruel present. There's only one person it could be.

Sirius. Every letter in that name sends a shiver down his spine.

Who else? Sirius responds.

He presses his lips together tightly. He thought he'd escaped this life. He thought he could run from it when he married Collette, as if stepping into her light could make all the dark parts of his past vanish.

I have an assignment for you.

I'm done with that life.

It's not done with you. Ominous, yet true. There's no viable way for him to hide this from Collette any more. His wife deserves to know who she really married.

Another text comes through.

Do you accept?

It would be easy to ignore Sirius, but he knows what will happen if he does. So he replies: *Who is the target?*

Details later tonight.

He shuts off his phone.

Dropping the groceries on the smooth gray counter, he calls for Colette. Her answering, "Here!" resounds faintly from the living room.

"What's up?" Colette looks up at him, tears spilling from her eyes, and hands him a positive pregnancy test. He grins. She's pregnant.

"You're pregnant!" He exclaims, forgetting all about Sirius for a moment. She nods, speechless with emotion, and he pulls her into a fierce hug. They've been trying for *so long*, and it's finally happened. They're going to be parents.

I'll tell her tomorrow, he thinks to himself. There's no way he could ruin this night with his news. He turns over in the bed towards his wife, but then he hears a ding. Sighing, he picks up his phone. And immediately drops it.

TARGET: COLETTE FRILL. DO YOU ACCEPT?

He *knew* this would happen one day, but he married Colette anyway. He'd ignored it, too deep in love to think of the consequences. There's no way he can tell her now. He clenches his jaw and gets out of bed as quietly as he can manage, then once he has locked himself in the bathroom, he calls the number. It connects.

"No," he says quietly, not bothering with a greeting.

"You know what will happen if the assignment is not completed," Sirius drawls.

"I know," he says, pinching the bridge of his nose painfully. "I know, and I can't do it. I can't kill her. I won't."

"It's not a question of whether, it's a question of when. You have until the baby is born."

"How did you-" he starts to ask, but the line disconnects and he's left staring at his phone in the house he shares with his soon-to-be-dead wife. He knows what will happen if he doesn't kill her. So he slides into bed and makes a vow to himself. *These last nine months of her life will be the best she's ever had.*

He keeps that vow.

They go to her favorite places when she's two months pregnant, and he takes endless pictures, knowing they'll be all he has left when she's gone.

Seven months.

They take a long plane ride when Colette's stomach has just started to swell, off to see a country she's dreamed of visiting since she was a little girl.

Five months.

When Colette's too tired to travel, he dotes endlessly on her. He kisses her belly and promises that their little girl is going to be just as fantastic as her mother. They didn't find out the gender, but he *knows* it's a girl. If Colette can't live, at least she can live on through their daughter.

Three months.

"You're going to be such an amazing father," Colette says drowsily one night, her head on his shoulder. He swallows the guilt, swallows the horrible reality of the future looming over them, and instead turns the channel.

One month.

Colette gives birth 5 weeks later, and he cries as she hands their child to him. It's a boy. *It doesn't matter,* he promises himself. It doesn't matter that it's not a girl. But it does. It does.

"You may have my face," he whispers to their son one night, "but I hope that is the only thing we share."

He pays a visit to a nice older couple the next day, and signs the papers. The adoption will be closed.

He gets a call.

"It's nearly time," Sirius says.

"I know."

"What are you waiting for?" The call ends. It's time.

He drops off their son at the older couple's house one afternoon, ignoring his own features and seeing only Colette's as he takes one last look at his son, then he goes home empty handed. He can hear Colette humming in the kitchen when he walks in, which makes it that much harder for what must happen next.

"Where's the baby?" she asks, not turning around.

"Gone." She turns at that.

"What do you mean, *gone*?" She looks hysterical.

"I mean safe. Safe in a way he never was with us."

"What do you mean? He was always safe with us, we're his *parents*!"

"No," he says quietly. "He was never safe, not when I am who I am." Colette looks confused. He continues.

"I was a hit man," he whispers. "For many years. I swear I retired, but I have one more assignment. And I have to complete it." Colette is shaking her head and he sees tears run down her cheeks.

"Who?" she asks, but he can tell she already knows. And he can't lie to her, not about this.

"You," he says softly, and pulls out a gun. Her eyes widen as he clenches his jaw with determination. She isn't crying anymore, she's standing up straight, as if she knew this day would come. Maybe she did. It wouldn't surprise him.

"I love you to the moon-"

"And back," she chokes, and he pulls the trigger. Her body slumps to the ground. He gets a call.

"Is it done?" Sirius asks. He feels empty, dead. He can barely say the next sentence with the repressed sobs building in his chest.

"It's done."

"Good. Are you planning to keep my grandson from me? It would be a shame if this situation had to repeat itself."

"No. He's away."

"In the next room while you killed his mother? Classy." "No. Adopted."

"Very good."

The call ends. One more shot rings throughout the house.

HARBORING HOPE: TAKING A LOOK AT HOMELESSNESS IN TRAVERSE CITY THROUGH THE LENS OF ONE ORGANIZATION, SAFE HARBOR

Lucy Poppleton, 11th grade

Honorable Mention for Journalism

TRAVERSE CITY—Near the Woodmere Branch of the Traverse Area District Library and the Boardman River is Safe Harbor, tucked away behind Eighth Street shops and businesses. At six o'clock each winter night, the doors open wide, welcoming guests inside after a day spent out in the cold. They check in at stations where staff and volunteers wait to receive them. Some are regulars who stay at Safe Harbor every night. Others are first timers there or at an emergency shelter in general. The guests roam over to the dining area, where volunteers are waiting to dish out delicious, hearty meals. After eating, guests can access a number of services from showers to laundry to the internet. They can also visit the heated yurt right outside for entertainment. In the morning, breakfast is provided to guests before they have to return to the streets.

Started in 2003 as a collaboration between various area churches, Safe Harbor has grown in scope and size, opening its physical location in 2017. Their goal is to care for homeless individuals in our community during the cold winter months from October to April. On any given night, around 200 people in the Grand Traverse area are experiencing homelessness. This number is too high for the size of the community we live in, but Safe Harbor has certainly helped. "This last year...we served over 290 different individuals throughout the season," tallies longtime Safe Harbor board member and volunteer Joshua Brandt. "We had over 10,000 bed nights. We had over 22,000 meals served." Beginning this winter season, Safe Harbor has expanded to be open all day Saturday and Sunday. Most important to service at Safe Harbor, though, is an emphasis on the word "guest." The shelter aims to create an environment where people experiencing homelessness are treated with as much dignity as possible, as they might not be awarded that same dignity in other areas of their lives. "They have somewhere to sleep where they can get a good night's rest and hopefully wake up the next morning rejuvenated and ready to face whatever they have to face that day," says Brandt kindheartedly.

Safe Harbor is just one part of a complex homeless response system in the Traverse City area. They are a part of the Northwest Michigan Coalition to End Homelessness (NWCEH), a group of organizations and agencies that helps those without homes. Their goal, outlines director Ashley Hallady-Schmandt, is to make "homelessness rare (so it doesn't happen very often), brief (so if it does happen for people, they can quickly get out of it), and one-time (so if someone becomes homeless, they never become homeless again)." The NWCEH works together to connect homeless people with resources to transition to more permanent homes. The Coalition includes bottom level safety nets such as Safe Harbor, housing resources, and meals throughout the day when shelters are closed. Collaboration is an essential part of the solution to homelessness. "[Safe Harbor is] trying, always, to do a better job of making information about the certain services that are available in town—other agencies and other organizations—available to the guests," describes Brandt.

A complex response is necessary for homelessness because homelessness is a complex issue. "There are different degrees of homelessness," describes community volunteer and former Missions Pastor Randy Burgess. Some people sleep outdoors, while others may stay in one of the emergency shelters in the area. "With youth, there are kids who surf around from friend's house to friend's house, and they're not in a tent out in the woods, but they don't have any stability," continues Burgess. Furthermore, Brandt explains that the idea that homelessness is more complicated than people might realize. "My personal awareness of the issue of homelessness and my personal compassion for folks that are experiencing homelessness [has increased]," reflects

Brandt upon his service at Safe Harbor. "[I have] a deepening understanding that it really can happen…a lot more easily than people realize."

In addition, once someone arrives in housing, they still need support. "[Exiting] homeless[ness] doesn't always solve all the problems. It's an important step, but the issues related to homelessness often continue even when people get housing," expresses Burgess. "[I] learned that these weren't just a few odd people in our community, but these people were our neighbors, and they're people, and they're people who have feelings and hopes and dreams," reflects Burgess. "I now have many of these individuals [as] lifelong friends."

For many high school students, homelessness is a complicated topic that we might not know much about. "I would want you to know that nobody is homeless on purpose. It's not that anybody sets out to say 'today, I'm going to leave my home and live this crazy life,'" Burgess advises. "There are always circumstances that have something to do with [homelessness], and a lot of times, those circumstances are out of people's control, and so they're finding themselves in a pretty chaotic time." The best way to approach the topic is to be compassionate, a friend who cares, and someone who can be present to others. If you would like to learn more about homelessness in the area or volunteer, you can contact an organization such as Safe Harbor.

Everyone, even high school students, can be a part of the solution.

If you or someone you know is experiencing homelessness, you can reach out to the homeless response hotline at +1 (844) 900-0500.

FINDING REFUGE
Kristen May, 12th grade
First Place in Journalism

When one looks into the Traverse City community, they will find a blend of many different cultures. The war in Ukraine has increased the amount of Ukrainian refugees seeking sanctuary in Traverse City. Whether they're a transfer student or someone who came here to get away from the war, there is a much larger Ukrainian community than there used to be.

If you're a Ukrainian living in Traverse City, it's nice to know that you're not alone and that there are others who may be experiencing the same emotions that you are. Dmytro P., a Ukrainian who came to Traverse City, says that, "Half of my time [I go to] Ukrainian church and [the] other time Living Hope. I like the people. I like how they do service. It's more like [a] Ukrainian church here." Going to church can give Ukrainians a sense of familiarity, which can make their transition to our city easier. Diana Y., another Ukrainian residing in Traverse City, also enjoys attending church. "I [go] to church and work groups." Being separated from your friends and family back home is hard when you're hours away, and it's so much worse when there are thousands of miles between you. "[I'm] usually [able to talk to them] once or twice a month...[sometimes I] become really worried, it's two weeks gone and I can't get ahold of them, and at the same time I try to tell myself that they don't have power, everything's good," Ukrainian exchange student Anastasiia Hrukach '23 explains. There's always a fear lurking in the back of your mind that is constantly asking, are they okay, are they safe, are they alive? For Hrukach, it's a constant struggle, but with the support of friends and family, she's not letting it overwhelm her. "I've lived with my second host family for more than a year now. I just love them," Hrukach comments. "They never had kids, but we became like a real family and I became their daughter. I feel really comfortable about them, and they've helped me so much."

It's been over a year since the war in Ukraine started, and there are still so many questions. What's happening over there, why is this happening, and most importantly, when will this horrific event end? The war has had a large and overreaching effect on so many parts of the world, even here in Traverse City. The Ukrainian community has been hit hard by the war, and it's impossible to know where to go from here, but they're not alone in their struggle. Traverse City's community is supporting them every chance they get and are finding ways to make their lives easier. One example is a bike ride called Ride for Peace, which "hit the trails to raise money for the World Central Kitchen...they've raised close to $3,000 for the World Central Kitchen who's been feeding Ukrainian refugees since the start of the war," according to 9&10 News. The events aren't only good to raise money; they're also a great opportunity to meet new people and form long-lasting friendships.

Even nationally-based organizations have stepped in to help. Bethany Christian Services is a "global nonprofit that supports children and families with world-class social services, all designed to help families thrive, who also has been involved with Ukrainian refugees," according to the Bethany Christian Services website. They're helping with the Ukrainian refugee crisis by providing support to Ukrainian refugees arriving in the US, whether that support comes as food, shelter, transportation, access to medical care, or any of the other dozen ways they're providing help. Allie Burritt, the Refugee Site Supervisor at Bethany Christian Services in Traverse City, notes that "we have three different programs that work with refugees and immigrant...we're working with people coming through the program called Uniting for Ukraine...then we have our refugee resettlement program which is for people who are also from Ukraine but they come with legal refugee status. They have a pathway to get to citizenship after five years." There are many ways for refugees to get to the United States, but even so, it's a struggle. Even if they manage to get to the U.S., they still have to find a place to stay, a job, etc. "Housing is very difficult to come by in Traverse and it's also very expensive. Transportation is really challenging too, they're relying on family members," Burritt points out. There's also an aspect of responsibility that falls to the people refugees are staying with. "The people coming through Uniting for Ukraine need to have a sponsor, someone who will care for them during the time that they're here. So a lot of this is relying on Ukrainian family members who themselves were refugees only a few years ago."

The future of Ukraine may be uncertain, but with the warm and welcoming community of Traverse City, Ukrainians are able to settle into a new home.

THE VALUE OF THE UNKNOWN
Isabelle Keely, 11th grade
Honorable Mention in Nonfiction

Regrettably, I have spent my entire life in fear. I have missed out on countless opportunities because of my crippling fear of the unknown. I have chosen a life of predictable comfort rather than embracing the unpredictable and experiencing some of the greatest joys of life that take place on the other side of fear. Despite my dreams of taking the world by its reins and making it mine for the taking, I have never been able to get past the initial anxiety of conquering the unknown to reach the joys of the other side. I often wonder, how has the trajectory of my life been altered by my anxiety? Had I conquered my fears growing up, where would I be today? As acclaimed author and aviator Anne Morrow Lingbergh once wrote, "We tend not to choose the unknown which might be a shock or a disappointment or simply a little difficult to cope with. And yet it is the unknown with all its disappointments and surprises that is the most enriching". There is an immeasurable value in taking risks, in spite of the unknown, to enjoy the pleasures of life on the other side of fear.

In the seventh grade, my school, along with thousands of other schools in the nation, planned our class trip to Washington D.C. It was mid-November, and the introduction of the trip the following August caused all of us to be buzzing with excitement. Beneath the surface of my awkward, braced smile I was screaming. Questions and uncertainties swarmed through my head at lightning speed, the unknown piercing my lungs with every breath I drew. I could not understand it; this was something I was supposed to look forward to. Instead, I felt as though I was a frightened Kindergartener again, tightly gripping my mother's coat, begging her not to leave me in such a frightening place. The D.C. trip brought back that familiar anxious feeling, this time-- ten fold. Throughout my seventh grade year, not a day went by that I didn't wake up with a sickening knot in my stomach about that trip. As the days of the trip drew nearer, the panic-like sensation only increased. So, consequently, while everyone FaceTimed one another and packed their bags, I was desperately trying to craft any excuse I could muster to tell my parents I could not go on the trip. My parents listened to my pleas, reluctantly, and assured me that I would gravely regret this decision later in life. As much as I knew they were absolutely right, the relief I felt of not attending the trip was all-consuming. However, as the following years went by, that sweet relief turned bitterly sour. Now, as a junior in high school, I am still surrounded by the remembrance of all of the things I missed out on from that trip. All of the inside jokes; all of the lifelong memories; all of the things I will never be a part of. While this feeling of regret has trickled into every aspect of my life through the years, it has taught me a valuable lesson. Simply put: I never want to feel that way ever again.

Thus came the winter of my junior year of high school. An opportunity --that later proved pivotal in my life-- is presented before me, completely mine for the taking. I have been invited to an Economic Summit, to meet various US congressional representatives and heads of Traverse City. At this conference, I am expected to represent my school, and more specifically the Michigan Youth in Government program, and to learn how to become more involved as a young person in the local community. When my father broke this news to me, I was ecstatic. All my life, I have always wanted to be involved with the change I want to see in the world, and this conference was a front row seat to get a taste of what I want to do with my life. At this conference, I would be introduced to individuals that truly have the power to make the change that I want to see, and I wanted to take advantage of that. The only thing in my way? The angst of the unknown. The feeling was back-- that same deafening screaming in my brain, telling me to fear the unknown; telling me to run away. But this time something was undoubtedly different; I didn't *want* to listen to that screaming in my head; I didn't want to let it overcome me as it had so many times before. Ignoring the gnawing feeling in my stomach, I accepted the invitation.

The conference itself was relatively manageable. I was expected to show up (quite snazzily dressed, might I add), shake some hands, and converse with some local officials, nothing I hadn't done before. As I walked shakily down the large staircase into the ballroom, I once again felt like a scared child, longing for her mother to hide behind. I made my way down the stairs, slapped on a name tag and bolted for the refreshment table. In my head, I thought having something in my hand to fiddle with would ease my anxiety and help me gather courage to speak to people. As I was introduced to more and more amazing people, my anxiety waned. I actually felt a sense of confidence; people wanted to speak to me because I was the only young person there. After about an hour of drifting conversations with many different people, we all made our way into the actual conference room, where a stage set with 4 chairs stood before us all. As everyone took their seats, the four panelists took the stage, and the questionnaire began. At first, I found myself rather relieved. I figured, now that other people are doing the talking, nothing is expected of me anymore, and I can just sit back and listen. However, in the back of my mind, I felt a buzzing-like sensation, almost calling me to stand up and become part of the conversation. In a spur of the moment, perhaps with no prior thought whatsoever, I shot my hand into the air and rehearsed a question frantically in my head. Before I had the chance to second guess my actions and place my hand back in my lap, the spokesperson gestured for me to stand up and ask my question. As if my mouth was completely independent from the rest of my body, I heard myself say (rather confidently), *As a young person, what is the best way for me to become more involved with our local economy and be a part of policy change?* As the panelists began to answer, I slowly sat back into my seat, completely amazed at my ability to push past my fears and taste freedom from my anxiety. As dramatic as it may sound, it was the aftermath of this moment that made me realize the value in pushing past my fears. I had representatives and their staff closing in from every direction, business cards in hand, offers on the tips of their tongues, waiting to speak with me. The most memorable of people, perhaps, being Senator Gary Peters' secretary, who offered me a summer internship at his office this coming summer; an opportunity I never would have had if I had not have stood up and asked that simple question. After hours of conversing with these people that once greatly intimidated me, I left that ballroom with more confidence than I had ever felt in my entire life. I felt as though I could do anything.

From the first days of kindergarten, to my Washington D.C. trip in seventh grade, all I have ever known is fear. However, despite this unreasonable fear of the unknown that has plagued me my entire life, I have regained control of my life, and regained a sense of confidence. Through ups and *many* downs, I have learned the immeasurable value in pushing myself beyond my fears; I have learned the importance of persevering through the disappointments and obstacles. As Anne Morrow Lindbergh once wrote, "It is the unknown with all its disappointments and surprises that is the most enriching". I can confidently say that I have never allowed myself to feel the way I did that summer of seventh grade; I wish I could go back in time and reassure myself that one day, I would be strong enough to enjoy my life rather than sitting back and watching it happen before me. I have spent the last four months learning how to trust. Learning to trust my surroundings, to trust in my ability to be resilient, to trust in myself to push past my fears for things I truly want. And now that I have trusted myself to see the beauty of life on the other side of fear; there is absolutely no going back.

DREAMS OF HOME
Taqwa Totakhail, 11th grade
First Place in Nonfiction

Saturday, August 14, 2021, was a big day. The day that changed my life, the day we moved to the U.S.A, just one day before the Taliban came to Afghanistan, destroying everything. How was it possible that the very next day, August 15, we arrived in a different world, the United States of America? And then just two days later, in Traverse City, Michigan. While we watched scenes of horror play out back home, I at least was safe. Embraced by a wonderful new family, Ann and Don Gregory, who gave us a place to stay – a refuge from which to relearn our lives. I was 15 years old.

After one month, my dad started the process to get us to school. At first, I thought that they would put me in 7th or 8th grade because I couldn't speak English at all. Then my dad said, "You're going to high school and the 10th grade." At first, I was nervous, excited, and kind of scared. I was outside of my safety zone. But I was thinking, "I can make it."

On the first day of school, I was so surprised. The students did not have uniforms. They were allowed phones in school. Boys and girls are in the same school and took classes together. In the classes, the students use computers more than books, including for doing their homework.. During exams, the teachers allowed the students to use textbooks and notes. On math exams, they could use calculators. All of this was very different from what I had known in Afghanistan.

I also found deeper cultural differences. In Afghanistan, teachers and principals are very serious and command respect from the students. This included hitting our hands with a stick or ruler when deemed "necessary". (Which happened frequently, in my experience!) Here, in contrast, the teachers and principals are more like friends with students, focused on finding ways to make things easier. So if a student needs any school materials, they can get it in class from the teacher or from the office. The students never have a hard time if they need pens, pencils, notebooks, or any other things – like help with homework or assignments. The most important thing here is that students be given every opportunity to learn – starting with the idea that they have to be safe. They have to be comfortable that their lives are safe. They must never think, "Am I going home alive or not?"

Afghanistan is the opposite of all of this. We have to wear uniforms. We are not allowed to have phones, or computers, or anything electronic in school. If the students do have these things, the teacher will take it or break it. We use books in classes all the time and we have to write a lot, sometimes six pages in one hour. For exams, we are allowed just one pen and one piece of paper. Our exams are very hard. We can't use any notes or textbooks. I remember having to memorize the answers to 200 questions in one night.

The teachers in Afghanistan are so serious that the students are afraid to talk with them. The principals are even more strict and often even the teachers can't talk with them! I remember that if the principals were in the hallway, no one could move from their chairs. The effect of this was to make learning very hard, but it also ensured that we did learn.

But perhaps the most striking difference between my experience in school here and in Afghanistan is about safety. Here, people are increasingly concerned about safety in the wake of gun violence. But thankfully this is not something that has affected most students. By contrast, students in Afghanistan deal with the threat of violence almost every day. I personally experienced an attack at a neighboring girls school that killed more than 1,000 students. I could hear the explosion and see the smoke from my school. It was terrifying. I can assure you that it's very hard to focus on learning when you're afraid.

Today under Taliban rule schools in Afghanistan have been shutdown and learning for girls has all but stopped. This means that more than half of the country is not in school (60% of Afghanistan's population is female). This includes in my own family all of my cousins who have been left in Afghanistan. More than 20 girls, some older and others younger than me. All stuck at home today, not able to go to school. They are harder workers than me but they have no future without an education. This is what the Taliban seems to want. Twenty years ago, the first time they were in power, the Taliban also closed schools. It was only after they were overthrown that a new generation, including my family, had the opportunity to study freely and to become successful. Today, the Taliban is trying once again to turn back the clock.

For me, the most important part of America is education. Education freedom. Education quality. And education opportunity for all. I feel that I have found an education home here that will allow me to make my own future. In contrast, education in Afghanistan is so hard and challenging – no access to schools for girls and the constant threat of violence. I am the lucky one. I am the safe one. I am home.

"AMONG THE WILDFLOWERS" AFTER KEVIN YOUNG

Megan Speers, 12th grade
HONORABLE MENTION IN POETRY

Praise the roadside ditches that you call your home
    the trail sides,
    the swamps, the beaches,
    the sandy, warm dunes.
Praise the patches where you grow up,
    purple and yellow,
    an array of complementary colors.

Praise the sun
    that refracts your lovely purple and gold colors.
Praise your delicate petals
    white or lilac or magenta
    held up by tall, spindly stems.
Praise your showy royal blossoms,
    layers of deep, rich purple petals, my favorite variety,
    September's daisies.
Praise your delicate yellow clusters.
    tiny flowers bunched together by the hundreds,
    golden stamens reaching out to be pollinated.

Praise the bees
    that buzz lazily
    around your colorful array,
    they rely on you,
    the last wildflowers of the season.

Praise the little mammals and birds
      that feed on your seeds
      in the dead of winter.

Praise your innumerable varieties,
      too many for the guidebooks to hold.

Praise your golden pollen,
      carried on the wind,
      it's too heavy to give me allergies.

      I wish I could spend every sunny October day
      laying among the asters and goldenrod.

GHAZAL WITH BUBBLEGUM AND BUZZING DOWNWARD THOUGHT SPIRALS WITH LYRICS FROM MARINA

Eli Pszczolkowski, 12th grade

First Place in Poetry

Past and future regrets stick around like bubblegum, buzz about in my
head, bees that sting again and again and buzz about

when I was blasting Marina in her car, thought I was the luckiest guy in
the world. Chewed me up and spat me out, 'cause that's what young love's
buzzing about.

It would never last forever, but I tripped over the chance, thought it
wouldn't pop my bubblegum heart, but that's what everyone buzzes about.

No time for that now, I've got a future ahead.

Try things out, cobble something together before I'm overseas buzzing
about

with my buzz cut and my camo pants, or chained to a restaurant chain
working back of house, coworkers call me Dish God before I buzz about

my buzz hut and hit another puff. Try, try to forget the time
when I knew I'd go farther, do better, when I could've still listened
to the bubblegum sticky stuck regrets that buzz about and about,
when the little beekeeper had room to buzz around and find out.

Contributors

Front Street Writers Creative Writing Lab Grand Traverse

Sela Geraci is a senior at Leland Public School, and will be attending Albion College the next fall semester. She has always enjoyed reading and has a passion for writing. One day she hopes she will have her own novel published and to continue to incorporate the art of storytelling into her life.

Delaney Cram is a senior at TC West High School and has been participating in the National Writers Series since middle school. She specializes in creative writing, but she has also been writing for her school's newspaper for two years. In her free time, Delaney enjoys reading and rowing. She plans on studying history and literature in college.

Tess Tarchak-Hiss is a freshmen at Traverse City West Senior High School. She has been writing seriously for two years, and plans on taking writing courses at The National Writers Series for her remaining years of highschool. She is primarily interested in creative nonfiction, and short stories.

Front Street Writers: Manistee

Lola Piper is a senior at Manistee High School. She will be starting at Grand Valley State University in the fall where she will study English Literature and Education.

Grace Condon is an eighth grader living in Manistee Michigan. From a large family, Grace enjoys writing and art. She moved to Michigan in 2020 after leaving Minnesota.

Alexis McClellan is an eighth grader at Manistee Middle School. She enjoys writing, painting and performing.

Leah McClellan is an eighth grader at Manistee Middle School. Reading is one of her favorite subjects at school.

Marlee Hamilton is a sixth grader at Manistee Middle School. She enjoys diving and playing baritone.

Jonas Carlson is a sixth grader at Manistee Middle School. Jonas enjoys photography and urban exploring. He enjoys computer games and local history.

Jacob Szynski is a sixth grader at Manistee Middle School. He enjoys exploring and learning about old building in the area. He plays trombone and enjoys skiing.

Leah Szynski is a sixth grader at Manistee Middle School. She enjoys swimming, reading, writing and spending time with her dog.

Tomas Racine is a sixth grader at Manistee Middle School. He loves writing stories and spending time at the Youth Armory Project.

Flash Fiction for Middle Schoolers

Kent Gardner Dickenson is a 7th grade student at Glenn Loomis Montessori. He is the founder and editor of The Weekly Guillotine. Aside from writing or reading a good story, he enjoys fencing, football and basketball.

Eliana Koller lives in Traverse City. She's a 6th grader at West Middle School (Go, Titans!) with her BFFAE Sophie. Eliana lives with her adorable younger brother Alex, her mom and dad, and a soon-to-be-novelized hamster. Her favorite color is dark turquoise and her favorite animal is a jackal. One final message from Eliana: READ!

JuJu Pine is in 6th grade and lives in Gaylord. If she isn't reading or writing, she is probably watching Stranger Things, playing softball, or hugging a cat! She can't wait to defend her team's title as the Otsego County Library's Battle Of the Books winner next year!

Sophie Schopieray lives in Traverse City with her mom, dad, brother Fin and dog Wally. She loves writing fantasies with her BFFAE, singing, playing piano, and making up weird names for people. Sophie hopes to publish a book by the time she's 20! She currently attends West Middle School with her best friend Eliana, and suffers from her sarcasm. Her favorite quote is: "Pity the living, and above all, those who live without love."

Building Stories

Liam Faunce has been a dedicated writer since childhood. Faunce is inspired by pop culture and A24 movies, and is currently trying to gather up the courage of writing a novel in either the categories of YA, Fiction, or Mystery-thrillers. Liam lives in Traverse City Michigan with three pets and family.

Kristen May is an 11th grader at Central High School. She has been writing since she was nine years old and has had several literary pieces published in the National Literary Journal. She lives in Traverse City with her family and golden retriever.

TADL's NWS Novel Writing Program

Jack Hennessy is the author of the in-progress novel *Divided We Fall,* as well as the in-progress stage play *Middle School Musical.* He is currently a student at Compass Montessori Junior High in downtown Traverse City. Jack plans to attend Interlochen Arts Academy in the fall to study Creative Writing. He lives in Traverse City, Michigan, with his parents, brother, cat (Scully), and tortoise (Quint).

Mina Cotner is a 10th grader at Central High School and grew up in the two worlds of Chicago and Northern Michigan and began weaving stories in elementary school. At the time of writing, his hobbies include the likes of "walking in the rain" and "making calls to nobody."Mina Cotner grew up in the two worlds of Chicago and Northern Michigan and began weaving stories in elementary school. At the time of writing, his hobbies include the likes of "walking in the rain" and "making calls to nobody."

Ingrid Waldron is 12 years old and spends her time reading, writing, drawing, and playing video games. She has one cat and three chickens.

Ava Hartley

Ava Audré Hartley lives in Traverse City, Michigan. She is 13 years old and enjoys her dogs, cats, and fish at home. She goes to Greenspire Middle School and loves the outdoor time she gets there.

Novel Writing Program at West Middle School

Sophia Eustice is a 7th grader and the author of the in-progress novel *Champion*. She loves to read amazing books like the Percy Jackson books (not the movies) and the Harry Potter books. She has seven crazy siblings that she loves to death and amazing friends. She loves to listen to 80's and 90's music and some 2000's. She is also in a great choir program that she loves in Traverse City. She also enjoys coding and building legos, and baking in her free time.

Mateo Nash is a sixth grader at West Middle School. When not writing, he enjoys reading, drawing, playing chess, and watching movies in his free time. He mainly draws dinosaurs, especially Tyrannosaurus, and Jurassic Park is both his favorite book and movie. His favorite food is sushi. He has lived in Traverse City for all twelve years of his lifetime, with his mother and father, Marian and Taylor, respectively, and his younger brother, Declan.

Abigail Reding is a sixth grader at West Middle School in Traverse City, MI. She lives with her parents, older sister Olivia, and goldendoodle Flynn. This is her first full-length novel, though she has written short stories on her own and with her sister, who is also a writer. She enjoys reading, drawing, baking, running, and listening to music.

Azraeya Dunham is 13-year-old 7th grader at Travers City West Middle School.

Writers Studio

Minnie Bardenhagen is Junior who attends Suttons Bay High School. She is a member of the Writers Studio program at Career Tech, and a finalist in the 2023 Young Playwrights Festival. She is a participant in the theater, choir, and band programs at her school, and aspires to become a music therapist.

Sydney Boettcher is a Junior at the Greenspire High School and Career Tech Writers Studio. He is a finalist in the 2023 Young Playwrights Festival. Next year he will be a foreign exchange student in Thailand.

Reegan Craker (they/he) is in 11th grade at Suttons Bay High School. They live in Northport and hope to complete a four-year degree in digital cinema and a two-year degree in illustration at Northern Michigan University. He enjoys writing stories and being able to creatively visualize them to showcase his works in every way possible.

Alister Easterwood (they/them) is a senior at Forest Area High School, as well as a second-year student in Writers Studio at Career Tech. They were a finalist of the 2022 Young Playwrights Festival. They enjoy poetry and playwriting.

Marisa Marshall is a 12th grader at Elk Rapids High School who has just started writing under the pen name M. J. Marshall. She wishes to be a publishing author in the future, her dream is to be a bestseller, and loves to write and read contemporary romance. Her plan after high school is to attend writing classes at a community college and work hard to save up money while continuing to work on her novels.

Randale McCuien is in 11th grade at Traverse City Central High School. He is often inspired by anime in his writing. He is greatly interested in theater arts and has a role in Central's production of *Into the Woods*. Music is a significant part of his day to day life.

Lucas McSwain is an 11th grade student from Traverse City Central High School attending NorthwestEd Career Tech, Writers Studio. He aspires to travel around the world and start off his career path in the United States Navy. Part of his want to travel includes writing about others experiences and perspectives as well as telling his own.

Dominic Montoya-Arlt, age 17, has lived in northwestern Michigan his entire life and doesn't plan on changing that fact anytime soon. He is eager to pursue a bone-chilling career as a librarian or in a related profession and will fill up his spare time with writing, tabletop games, and vomiting out words in a vague approximation of singing.

Mason Moran is a musician and writer from Traverse City, Michigan. He has been learning about writing in the Career Tech Writers Studio program. He is interested in performing in musical theatre and playing video games.

Abraham Murphy lives in northern Michigan with his five siblings and his parents. He helps tend his family's farm and enjoys creating poetry while in the sun. He has a love of fantasy and wishes to write a series involving fantasy elements.

Eli Pszczolkowski is a senior at Traverse City Central High School, and is preparing to ship off to Grand Valley State University to pursue screenwriting. He enjoys playing violin, taking care of his plants, and running outrageous games of D&D with friends. Some of his favorite stories include *The Magnus Archives*, Avatar: The Last Airbender, and *Over the Garden Wall*.

Vincent Redman is a Traverse City Central High School junior attending Career Tech's Writers Studio Program. In the future, he wants to become a psychiatrist and finds an acute interest in psychology. Aside from reading and writing, Vincent spends his free time playing video games.

Madeline Rowney (she/they) is a junior at Traverse City Central High School. Originally from England, Madeline spends most of her time writing and playing video games. She is a 2023 winner of the Young Playwrights Festival, and hopes to pursue a career in journalism.

Isabel Schmidt is a junior at Suttons Bay High School. She is an avid reader and writer who enjoys fiction the most. Isabel is planning to go to college and pursue writing in one way or another.

Megan Speers is a senior at Traverse City Central High School and lives in Fife Lake. Her favorite genres are poetry and creative nonfiction. She also enjoys environmental writing. Megan competed in the Michigan state Poetry Out Loud competition as the 2023 Writers Studio champion. After she finishes high school she plans to go to college to study environmental science.

Alicia Streeter is a student at Career Tech and Traverse City Central High School. They grew up in Michigan and enjoy the plethora of nature. They're a writer and artist who focuses on fiction and character creation.

Yahir Torres is a student in the Writers Studio program at the Traverse City Career Tech that also attends Kingsley Area Highschool. He's in his senior year and is looking at going to college down state to experience something new. He enjoys skateboarding, photography and being with friends in his free time.

Gabrielle Vermilya is a junior at Buckley Community High School, which she has been attending since preschool. She was never much of a reader, until the COVID-19 pandemic and she was trapped at home with her current favorite book, *The Wolf Wilder* by Katherine Rundell. A semifinalist in the Young Playwright's Festival with her play *Teenage Drama*, you can now find her reading classics like *Anna Karenina* by Leo Tolstoy, *Watership Down* by Richard Adams, or writing what she hopes will be a future bestseller.

Aubrey West is a junior attending Traverse City High School, who also attends Career Tech Writers Studio. Aubrey has been writing since she was little and eventually grew a strong passion for it, hoping to turn it into a career as a novelist. Her other interests include being a hobbyist with education, writing a yearbook entirely alone for her school, soon finding opportunities with college, and staying close to home in adulthood.

NWS Scholarship Winners and Honorable Mentions

Nevaeh Wharton is currently a senior at Traverse City Central High School who is preparing to go to college in the fall. She plans to attend college in New York City to continue to pursue many of her passions consisting of reading, writing, and psychology. In her free time, she often finds herself in front of a computer working on her book. From a young age, she developed an interest in reading and throughout the years she began wanting to write a book of her own. Maintaining her thirteen-year-old dreams and visions she is nearing the end of her editing process and hopes to publish her book sometime in the future.

Lucy Ettawageshik is the second oldest of eight children, and comes from a family of aspiring writers. She is a homeschooled senior and plans to attend Northern Michigan University in the fall, where she will be pursuing an English degree. Academics aside, she enjoys writing, reading, singing, listening to music, and playing volleyball with her family.

Lucy Poppleton is a junior at Traverse City Central High School. She is a content editor and staff writer for the *Black & Gold Quarterly*, Central's student-run magazine. Beyond journalism, Lucy is an avid reader and a diligent student. She plays travel softball, participates in track and field, and volunteers for the shelter about which her article was written.

Isabelle Keely is an 11th grade student at Elk Rapids High School and enjoys reading and writing during her free time. She hopes to study Social Affairs and Policy in college and travel the world.

Taqwa Totakhail is a 17-year-old student at Traverse City West Senior High School. Barely escaping the Taliban, Taqwa arrived in the United States from Kabul, Afghanistan, in August 2021 with her parents and four brothers. She arrived knowing some English, but had to quickly adapt to a new culture, a new climate, and a new language. Taqwa values her family and her faith whole-heartedly. While she is aware that females in Afghanistan are no longer allowed to attend school or hold many jobs, Taqwa treasures her opportunities now that she is in the United States. She is currently in the National Honor Society at T.C. West Senior High School and is studying Health Sciences at the Career Tech Center. Her dream is to become a doctor, specializing in internal medicine. Taqwa is extremely grateful for her parents' strength, faith, and support; and she is forever thankful for all of the people who have supported her along her journey.

Acknowledgements

NWS's Raising Writers programs—from scholarships to Battle of the Books and Poetry Workshops—are made possible by private donations, sponsors, and grants from the Michigan Arts and Culture Council, the National Endowment for the Arts, and the Dragonfly Fund.

We are deeply grateful to all of those who have supported our Raising Writers programs. Without countless hours from volunteers, donations, and the kindness of our community, these programs would not be possible.

The *NWS Literary Journal* is a team effort. Thank you to Mission Point Press and Andrea Reider for the book design; our NWS instructors, Jacque Burke, Lauren K. Carlson, Kevin Fitton, Karin Killian, and Teresa Scollon, thank you for your time and energy in making this special volume possible for students. Thank you to Gina Thornbury and the Grand Traverse Regional Community Foundation for their partnership and support in this year's NWS scholarship winners.

And, of course, thanks to all of the young writers who worked so hard on their entries and had the courage to share these words with the public.

Thank you to all!

Made in United States
North Haven, CT
03 May 2023